CHILD-CENTRED EDUCATION AND ITS CRITICS

JOHN DARLING

P·C·P

Paul Chapman
Publishing Ltd

Paul Chapman Publishing Ltd
144 Liverpool Road
London
N1 1LA

British Library Cataloguing in Publication Data

Darling, John
Child-centred Education and Its Critics
I. Title
370.1

ISBN 1 85396 2252

Typeset by Hewer Text Composition Services, Edinburgh

A B C D E F G H   9 8 7 6 5 4

CONTENTS

ACKNOWLEDGEMENTS

The thinking which this book represents owes much to conversations over a period of years with colleagues in Aberdeen and elsewhere. I am particularly conscious of debts to John Nisbet, Nigel Dower, Walter Humes and Joyce Watt. I would also like to record my appreciation of Margaret Sinclair's secretarial skills.

Some of the arguments in this book have already appeared in article form, and I am grateful for permission to use material from the following sources:

Darling J., (1982) Education as horticulture: some growth theorists and their critics, *Journal of Philosophy of Education*, Vol. 16, no. 2, pp. 173–85; Darling J., (1985) Understanding and religion in Rousseau's 'Emile', *British Journal of Educational Studies*, Vol. 23, no. 1, pp. 20–34; Darling J., (1990) The child-centred revolution in Scotland, *Education 3–13*, Vol. 18, no. 1, pp. 8–13; Darling J., (1990) Progressivism and individual needs, in N. Entwistle, (ed.) *Handbook of Educational Ideas and Practices*, Routledge, London, pp. 43–51; Darling J., (1993) The end of primary ideology, *Curriculum Studies*, Vol. 1, no. 3.

John Darling is a lecturer in education at the University of Aberdeen. He has taught philosophy and education in various universities and colleges, and has also taught in primary schools. He has published numerous articles on the philosophy of primary education and on theories of child-centred teaching and learning.

INTRODUCTION

In modern times there are opposing views about the practice of education. Some find such disagreement exasperating and long for a time when there were no disputes about education. But to discover such a period, how far back would one have to go? The first sentence in this paragraph is borrowed verbatim from Aristotle's *Politics*, written in the fourth century BC – and Western educational theory does not go back much further than that. The truth is that except where society remains static, educational change is ever present and, with it, debate about whether these innovations are sound.

This book is about one such development and a particular critique which this encountered. The development is the child-centred challenge to traditional practice in the British primary school, famously signalled by the Plowden Report. The counter-challenge which is to be examined is the critique of child-centred education put forward in the writing of a group of philosophers of education led by R. S. Peters. It will be argued that this critique weakened resistance to the subsequent political and populist pressure on the child-centred approach.

In part, this book is an explanation of one educational dispute in the 1960s and 1970s, and of the innovative theory and practice which preceded it. But the approach goes beyond the historical. This book is itself disputatious: it analyses the philosophers' critique and finds it unpersuasive. Part of the strategy for re-examining the philosophical challenge will be to ensure that the philosophers are seen in their intellectual and institutional context.

This book itself, of course, is written in a particular context. It is theoretical work produced at a time when influential voices are raised against educational theory, now disdainfully viewed as a way of mystifying the common-sense activity that we call 'teaching'. This is symptomatic of a climate in which the professions are coming under critical pressure while business and politics are in the ascendant. A current theme among politicians, industrialists and others who are dissatisfied with current educational practice is that schooling has lost touch with the 'real world' (a concept which is itself interestingly metaphysical). The schooling process is said to suffer from having an inadequately defined end-product. The process, and therefore the product, should be improved through a system of quality control involving (among other things) attainment targets and the testing of pupils from an early stage. Schools are adjured to concern themselves more with the needs of industry. Teachers who are unwilling to think along such lines are seen as myopic sentimentalists who must be brought to their senses and made to recognize their obligations to the nation's economy. After all, it is ultimately successful business ventures which create the wealth which makes our expensive school system possible.

This climate has allowed governments to play an increasingly directive role in education. Thirty years ago a minister's job was to prise large sums for the education service from the Treasury and to expand the numbers of teachers entering the profession. One of Margaret Thatcher's most memorable battles as an education minister some decades ago was over the supply of free school milk. Today governments concern themselves directly with the curriculum which they deal with in bluff 'no-nonsense' terms. The introduction of the National Curriculum (by a government pledged to reduce government power) represents an extension of government power almost unimaginable to those working in the education service before the 1980s.

All this puts child-centred education under pressure. It also creates a perplexing climate for primary teachers who were once fairly confident about where they were trying to go. For twenty-five years a sense of direction had been provided for primary schools by the idea of child-centred education. Should these guiding principles be re-established in the teeth of prevailing winds, or was child-centred education after all a mistake?

This book cannot produce complete answers to these questions, but it hopes to make some helpful contributions. It seems important, firstly, to re-examine child-centred education and its philosophical roots. Today's child-centred thinking will be shown to be the fruition of ideas developed by philosophers like Rousseau and Dewey. How were these ideas adapted, and why were they eventually given a large measure of acceptance? These are the concerns of the first part of the book.

The next, more analytical, part focuses on what many teachers have seen as a serious intellectual challenge to child-centred education. Part of the academic training undergone by many of today's teachers has been an exposure to the writings of R. F. Dearden, R. S. Peters and Paul Hirst. These philosophers are critical of child-centred thinking, and their writing has done much to cast doubts on its intellectual credentials. This book appraises such criticism and finds it of limited cogency.

Finally, the book analyses the changed position of child-centred education which now appears to be under siege. A convenient indicator of the tensions generated by such change is the fate of a Scottish report in the mid-1980s which recommended extending some features of child-centred primary practice into the early stages of secondary schooling (PDC, 1986). This was rejected by the government on the grounds that the report was based on the psychology of the individual child, whereas 'a society where enterprise and competition must be increasingly valued . . . must be a main determinant of what schools teach' (*TESS*, 1988, p. 1).

In the face of this kind of pressure, what is the future for child-centred education, and for the distinctive style which it has bestowed on primary education? The Hadow Report declared in 1931 that 'The primary school has its own canons of excellence and criteria of success; it must have the courage to stand by them' (Consultative Committee, Board of Education, 1931, p. xxvi). Today, courage may not be enough.

1

CHILD-CENTRED EDUCATION

What are we talking about? The book's first task must be to give some kind of account of what is involved in child-centred education or (to give it its convenient historical name) educational 'progressivism'. Once this is adequately set out we can proceed to the philosophical criticism to which it has been subjected, to an appraisal of this criticism, and to an examination of the new climate to which it has contributed. This chapter expounds child-centred education in fairly common-sense school-related terms, while subsequent chapters explore more philosophical expositions.

Suppose that a primary school is visited by someone whose only previous experience of primary education has been as a pupil in the 1950s or earlier. The first surprise to register with such a visitor may be the sound emerging from the school. Primary education used to be conducted in silence: all that could be heard were teachers' voices. Today there are audible signs of activity and discussion. Entering a classroom, today's visitor sees that children are sitting round tables or have their desks pushed together in a way that facilitates conversation. Partly this shows the teacher's recognition that social intercourse is natural: prohibition is inappropriate and seems, at least for much of the time, unnecessary. Partly the teacher may view pupil interaction as an educationally profitable enterprise – 'working together', a skill which more traditional forms of schooling have tended to neglect except on the games field.

There is a second way in which communication has become easier. Teachers are less likely to be held in awe by their pupils than they used to be. This reduction of the psychological barrier between teacher and taught means that children are less reluctant to ask for help with difficulties and at the same time can make decisions and take initiatives on their own without fear of repercussions. Permission need not be sought for moving from one's seat for legitimate purposes like the consultation of books. More generally, the absence of fear means that it is easier for the teacher to build good personal relationships with the pupils.

These new patterns of classroom life reflect a more fundamental change in the way education is conceived: they are the practical tip of the iceberg of progressive educational theory. This theory is not a new one. The earliest fully developed version was expounded by Jean-Jacques Rousseau in *Emile* in 1762 in which Rousseau declared that 'Nature provides for the child's growth in her own fashion, and this should never be thwarted' (p. 50). This approach to thinking about children and their education was taken forward by such writers as Pestalozzi and Froebel, John Dewey and William Kilpatrick. Each of these writers knew of the work of his predecessors, and developed or revised, sometimes quite critically, what had already been said. In Britain the influence of these thinkers beyond the world of ideas was for a long time very limited. From the 1920s, however, increasing numbers of people working in the school system were becoming interested, until in the 1960s the child-centred philosophy was publicly endorsed by official reports of which the best known are *Primary Education in Scotland* (the Primary Memorandum) (SED, 1965) and *Children and their Primary Schools* (the Plowden Report) (CACE, 1967).

Child-centred (or 'progressive') educational theory has to be understood as stemming from radical dissatisfaction with traditional practice. A necessary preliminary, therefore, to producing an intelligible outline of child-centred education is to bring to mind the nature of the traditional, subject-centred, teacher-directed approach to education – or at least the nature of this approach as it is portrayed, fairly or otherwise, by progressives themselves. In terms of curriculum content this is taken to involve first the systematic imparting of basic skills in language and numerical calculation, followed by instruction in a range (usually broad at first and narrow later) of established school subjects. Mastery of factual information is emphasized. In pedagogical terms the traditional approach involves the teacher expounding the subject and instructing the whole class at once. Pupil motivation depends on compliance and competition: there is no resort to devices which might convert tedium into fun. Gritty application and memory work are regarded as unavoidable and perhaps as constituting beneficial preparation for adult life.

The variety of critical reactions to this picture means that no definitive account of child-centred education can be given. Instead, the preliminary outline which follows identifies some central, recurring themes in the alternative tradition. It shows the kind of ideas and arguments that one might expect to find in a proponent of progressivism.

As a starting point, progressives see themselves as having taught us an appreciation of children as individuals. Their focus is less on what each might become and more on what each already is. This does not, however, entail a static conception of education. Indeed, quite the reverse: progressive writing exudes an awareness of children's growth and development. In child-centred education, however, children's educational development is not understood in terms of things that should be known, rules that must be followed, or adult characteristics that ought to be adopted. Children's development is seen as a gradual and 'natural' progression which is best aided by adults who have an appreciation of and a respect for the ways of children. Childhood, it is insisted, is not a defective version of adulthood: if it were, all schooling would have to be thought of as one long remedial course. Sometimes progressivism's positive valuing of the state of childhood has been coupled with a relative devaluing of adulthood; and perhaps it does no harm for educators to be reminded of some of the demerits of adult character and adult society. In *Democracy and Education*, Dewey observes, 'with respect to sympathetic curiosity, unbiased responsiveness, and openness of mind, we may say that the adult should be growing in childlikeness' (Dewey, 1916, p. 50).

Further, progressives emphasise that it is in the nature of the child to be active. Traditionalists are seen either as being unaware of this central characteristic, or as seeing it as something regrettable, or as preferring not to take it into account in their approach to education. This neglect can be seen in simple form in the insistence that children remain seated at their desks for most of the school day. More serious, perhaps, is the treatment of children as *mentally* inactive, as the passive (and often reluctant) recipients of knowledge provided by teachers.

The progressive view is that education should be designed to reflect the nature of the child. Importance is therefore attached to the study of children. The findings of educational psychology as well as common observation are seen as showing that, contrary to the assumptions implicit in traditional practice, children are intellectually curious, keen to find things out, and actively engaged in making sense of the world they live in. This picture explains why progressives prefer to think of education in terms of 'natural' development: the nature of the child, it seems, is geared towards learning.

Another side of this claim about children is that they are natural doers, makers and creators. Schools should cater for this by providing opportunities and materials for a range of physical activity and creative work. This has been much taken to heart in primary schools in one very obvious way: the provision for artwork. Displays of paintings in classrooms and corridors show the positive value attached to children's work. Child-centred teachers expect such painting to be 'spontaneous' rather than created by the conscious application of taught technique. This reflects their favourable estimation of each child's inherent talents, and their regard for the way the personality of each is expressed.

Child-centred education is not just a respecter of childhood, but a respecter of individual children and their differences. Diversity is welcomed as something that makes life richer: hence there is in progressivism a built-in suspicion of the kind of schooling which puts pressure on children to conform. According to the Plowden Report, children should be allowed 'to be themselves' (CACE, 1967, p. 187).

Where does this leave the teacher? If all this developing, discovering and creating is going to take place anyway, are teachers still necessary? There are, at the very least, implications for teachers which point to the need for a change in style. Their job can no longer be one of imparting a fixed body of valuable knowledge. If education is to be essentially a response to the enquiring mind of the child, the teacher's role would be better understood as one of research consultant or manager of resources. In American terminology, the teacher becomes primarily a 'facilitator'. As with any kind of investigative learning, this approach requires that children be given considerable freedom and independence. Learning cannot be interpreted as 'finding out for oneself' if the learner is always to be confined to a desk or even to a classroom.

It is about this point in child-centred educational theory that some teachers begin to feel that the pedagogical implications fail to match reality as they experience it. Many children in classrooms do not display eagerness to learn, nor do they respond positively to the opportunities which teachers provide for them. Teachers often feel compelled to resort to incentives and disincentives, to a system of sticks and carrots: their experience convinces them that abandoning these strategies for a liberal, non-authoritarian regime would produce a classroom situation where little of educational value occurred. Recognizing the substance of the sceptic's reaffirmation of the reality of life in so many classrooms, progressives offer two different diagnoses of what they see as a pathological situation. Both explanations attempt to reconcile the child-centred claim that children have a natural intellectual curiosity with the feeling that in school children are often minimally motivated.

The first claim is that children become reluctant learners because of their experience of schooling. Child-centred pedagogy cannot readily be introduced with a class of children who have previously been exposed to traditional teaching. Even without actually experiencing authoritarian and didactic approaches, children come to school with the expectation that they will receive instruction and will not be able to do as they see fit: parents tell them this, and the whole image of school in our culture transmits this message. Once children see education as something that other people do to them, so it is argued, they lose the ability to take any initiative or responsibility for their own learning.

The second explanation is given in curricular rather than in pedagogical terms. There is said to be a mismatch between what children want to find out and what teachers think they ought to learn. In particular the kinds of enquiry that children naturally pursue are not reflected in the way traditional schooling categorizes knowledge into different 'subjects'. It is this lack of correspondence which accounts for children's low motivation. Under the influence of this idea, many primary schools moved some distance away from a subject-based curriculum at least in the sense that they abandoned timetabled periods with bells ringing every forty minutes. The primary curriculum became much more fluid and flexible, with the interdisciplinary 'project' a significant vehicle for enquiry-based learning in many classrooms. But if subject boundaries are to be collapsed or ignored, is there a new guiding principle for shaping the curriculum?

The child-centred answer is that if the school is to be made to fit the child rather than the other way round, the curriculum should be determined by the child's needs and interests. The theoretical difficulties inherent in this dictum will be discussed in detail at a later stage. But there are practical difficulties as well. If twenty or thirty children were all to pursue individual interests, it would be difficult for a teacher to support and monitor their learning, or to accommodate the enlarged freedom which these activities would require. On the other hand, if it is true that in such a situation children would be eager to learn, teachers would theoretically be relieved of the burden of having to coax and nag children into intellectual activity. The exercise of authority would be little required except for sorting out the kind of interpersonal difficulties that arise from time to time within any institutional group. So child-centred educational theory suggests that we could and should have classrooms where learning is largely self-motivated and the atmosphere is fairly relaxed.

This is the practical vision of child-centred education. But underpinning this lies a set of ideas about the nature of children, the nature of knowledge and the nature of life itself. This is what justifies us in referring to a child-centred, or progressive, 'philosophy'. To acquire an adequate understanding of child-centred education, it will be necessary now to examine this philosophy and its development.

2

ROUSSEAU REVISITED

We begin not at the starting point, because in intellectual history there can be no such thing as a starting point. But if Jean-Jacques Rousseau cannot be seen as the founder of child-centred educational theory, he was unquestionably the most brilliant of its early exponents. Earlier, John Locke, in his earnest and pedestrian way, advanced many suggestions for enlightened teaching. With minimal acknowledgements, Rousseau developed some of these into a complete system and presented it dramatically in an imaginative package.

Emile is an account of the development of a fictitious eponymous pupil who is in the care of a tutor (effectively Rousseau himself). The guiding principle throughout is that what is to be learned should be determined by an understanding of the child's nature at each stage of his development. Besides arguing that this leads to a new approach to education, *Emile* was instrumental in advancing a new view of children which has, for good or ill, lasted down to the present day. Children are seen as very different from adults: they are innocent, vulnerable, slow to mature, and entitled to freedom and happiness. The book also contains some social and political philosophy, a short treatise on religion, and Rousseau's views on the place of women.

Its publication had an electrifying effect. Women particularly admired it. Such was the demand that booksellers found it less profitable to sell the book than to rent out copies by the hour. And it received the ultimate publicity boost of being sentenced to burning in the streets of Paris.

Emile makes a powerful emotional appeal to adults by portraying childhood in a way that has since become clichéd as 'the age of harmless mirth' (Rousseau, 1762, p. 43). Education and child-rearing, Rousseau thought, should do nothing to change this agreeable condition: children's fun should not be unnecessarily curtailed; they should not be subjected to threats, punishments and other vexations. Rousseau here uses one argument which is hardly open to today's child-centred theorists: one never knows how long a child may be given to live, and it is hardly fair to subject them to discipline for their future good when they may never reach adulthood (*ibid.*, p. 43). Perhaps this argument belongs uniquely to a period when, encouraged by writers like Rousseau, parents were making an increasingly strong emotional investment in their children even though the infant mortality rate was still high. In any case, Rousseau relates the point not just to the happiness of children but to the happiness of parents as well when he advises, 'Fathers, can you tell when death will call your children to him? Do not lay up sorrow for yourselves by robbing them of the short span which nature has allotted to them' (*ibid.*, p. 43).

A recurring theme in *Emile* is that individual children vary: Rousseau insists on the need to take stock of this. After all, we are told, the reason why sermons and lectures are invariably ineffective is that they are delivered to groups of people all of whom have their own peculiar bent (p. 284). The implication clearly is that education needs to be individualized. To become successful, we must study individual pupils, observing their expressions (pp. 187–8) and watching them at play (p. 58). 'Every mind has its own form' (p. 58); and, in personality terms, people are seen as developing 'countless differences of character' (p. 187).

At one level, then, Rousseau is very aware of individual differences and keen to stress the need for these to be given due heed. But, none the less, in the course of *Emile*, he develops a general picture of the nature of the child. This picture he sees as incompatible with traditional educational practice, and it is one which still influences educational thought. We can identify several crucial features in his account.

The first is that Rousseau sees the child having some fundamental impulse to activity. To begin with, this manifests itself in the need for physical mobility. 'Children,' Rousseau says, 'will always do anything that keeps them moving freely' (p. 105). But this restlessness is in time replaced by curiosity: mental activity is seen as a natural development of bodily activity (p. 130). To the teacher this may sound too good to be true. But Rousseau is quick to point out that the child's need to find out about things may bear little relation to the kind of enquiry that the teacher has traditionally favoured. Rousseau imagines what would happen if a scientist were exiled with his books and equipment to a desert island: 'he would scarcely trouble himself about the solar system, the laws of attraction, or the differential calculus. He might never even open a book again; but he would never rest till he had explored the furthest corner of his island' (p. 130).

A distinction needs to be made, therefore, between the desire for learning for the sake of learning, and the desire to find out about things that affect oneself and one's well-being. Only the latter is natural: instinct prompts us to explore our own worlds. Young children's educational programmes should, in Rousseau's view, be confined to those things in which they have a natural interest (p. 130). Underpinning this argument lies Rousseau's conviction that nature has implanted in the child certain instincts for the purpose of promoting development (p. 50). So there is more than sentiment in Rousseau's advocacy of an indulgent attitude to the characteristic activities of childhood: to restrain the promptings of nature is to restrict the child's growth. 'Let us lay it down as an incontrovertible rule that the first impulses of nature are always right' (p. 56). One application of this is that children should be free to move around, to play, and to explore.

Rousseau saw young people growing through a series of developmental stages, and the technique most suitable for the handling of one stage would not necessarily be appropriate to another. Yet the need to respect nature's intentions was an unchanging principle. Thus at the baby stage, breast-feeding was right and swaddling was wrong: attempts to improve on nature's plans were always suspect.

Thinking in these terms is made easier by Rousseau's belief in a divine designer. 'God made all things good', and this includes human beings, whose 'true' or 'real' nature is pure and uncorrupted. Corruption was inevitable, however, in modern city life. Consequently Emile was to be reared in an isolated, controlled rural environment, to be returned to mainstream society once his character had developed to the point where it was no longer vulnerable to malign influence. This idea resurfaced in early twentieth-century Britain in the progressive boarding schools (see Chapter 4) which pioneered child-centred policies: these were often founded in secluded locations where reformed ideas and values could flourish without contamination.

The second striking feature, therefore, in Rousseau's account of childhood is his conviction that children are naturally good. To understand this idea we must attend to the historical context in which Rousseau was writing. Rousseau's claim that there is no viciousness inherent in human nature (p. 56) is intended as a rebuttal of the doctrine of original sin. This theological notion was widely accepted; and it prompted, or was used to justify, a strictly disciplined approach to education. An illuminating example of this style of thinking is to be found in the ideas of John Wesley, the founder of Methodism and a contemporary of Rousseau's. Wesley thought that children should be made to realize 'that they are fallen short of that glorious image of God, wherein they were first created; that they are not now, as they were once, incorruptible pictures of the God of glory . . . but more ignorant, more foolish and more wicked, than they can possibly conceive' (Greven, 1973). Wesley's advice on how to deal with these self-willed creatures was thoroughgoing: 'Break their wills betimes, begin this work before they can run alone, before they can speak plain, perhaps before they can speak at all. Whatever pains it costs, break the will if you would not damn the child' (Southey, 1820, II, p. 304). The pain referred to here is, of course, the child's not the parent's! Wesley recommended whipping from the child's first birthday. Parents could doubtless reassure themselves with the appropriate Biblical text: 'Thou shalt beat him with the rod, and shalt deliver his soul from hell' (Proverbs 23:14). Breaking their wills involved preventing children from doing whatever they wanted. Life had to be lived from a sense of duty, and certainly not according to one's inclinations. For the promptings of nature were, for Wesley, suspect. 'The bias of nature,' he declared, 'is set the wrong way: education is designed to set it right' (Body, 1936, p. 56). This is the antithesis of Rousseau's view, and the approach to education which it supported renders quite intelligible the importance Rousseau attached to his ideas about the unsullied character of children.

One problem inherent in Rousseau's position is clearly that it needs to be reconciled with the mischief and malice that are sometimes evident in children's behaviour. This challenge Rousseau is prepared to meet in his general declaration that 'the how and why of the entrance of every vice can be traced' (Rousseau, 1762, p. 56). The details of these entrances need not detain us now, but it is important to note that we have here an early version of the invoking of external influences as the kind of explanation that explains things away: where apparently malicious behaviour is accounted for by pointing to causes or malign influences, the agent is effectively absolved of responsibility for the wrongdoing. The power of environmental influence is always to the fore in Rousseau's educational thought, though it is not seen, as it has been by some writers, as having the potential to provide a complete explanation. After all, if children were what circumstances made them, there could be no such thing as 'the child' or the child's 'nature'.

Rousseau's developmental account of this nature serves to underline the differences between children and adults. In particular, Rousseau drew attention to the dissimilarities in their powers of thought and focused on the limited nature of the child's understanding. This is the second key idea in Rousseau's account of childhood and one that has been, supported by the work of Piaget, a continuing influence on educational practice. This is how Rousseau put it: 'Childhood has its own ways of seeing, thinking, and feeling: nothing is more foolish than to try and substitute our ways; and I should no more expect judgment in a ten-year-old child than I should expect him to be five feet high' (*ibid.*, p. 54). But what is this power of judgement? Rousseau apologizes for any confusion that his account creates when, at a later stage, he declares, 'I am far from thinking . . . that children have no sort of reason' (*ibid.*, p. 72). But, in fact, clues to Rousseau's meaning are to be found at various points (pp. 72, 90, 122, 165–6). Here his thinking takes place in the context of the classical empiricist view that 'everything that comes into the human mind enters through the gates of sense' (p. 90). In the first instance, information is passively received in the form of sensations. Association of individual sensations produces simple ideas, which are also sometimes referred to as 'complex sensations' (p. 166); and this outcome is the result of an act of judgement in which one sensation is compared with another. This judgement is described by Rousseau as the reason of sense experience. But, as a further step, simple ideas can themselves be compared, which results in complex ideas. This is the sphere of the reason of intellect. Children, whilst born with only a capacity for sensations, acquire the first kind of reason, but not the second. This is the explanation for Rousseau's apologetic (and rather unhelpful) footnote: 'Sometimes I say children are incapable of reasoning. Sometimes I say they reason cleverly. I must admit that my words are often contradictory, but I do not think there is any contradiction in my ideas' (p. 72). The *kind* of reasoning which can be executed is what matters. Children can exercise judgement on what is within their own experience, but not on what is beyond their experience.

This leads directly to the key idea in Rousseau's treatment of learning. There is no difficulty in identifying the point because Rousseau himself has marked the place for every reader. The child, he writes, 'should remain in complete ignorance of those ideas which are beyond his grasp. My whole book is one continued argument in support of this fundamental principle of education' (p. 141).

Traditionally, teachers' expectations have been unreasonably high, with failure to learn being attributed to perversity and rewarded accordingly. The force of Rousseau's approach is to make us aware of the kind of understanding that the child can achieve at different levels: 'I cannot too strongly urge the tutor to adapt his instances to the capacity of his scholar' (p. 144). This involves rethinking what can be understood at which stage of the child's development. In his preface to *Emile* Rousseau complains, 'The wisest writers devote themselves to what a man ought to know, without asking what a child is capable of learning' (p. 1). Instead, Rousseau argues, the study of the child should be made the foundation on which a sound education is built, and such a study shows that much of the subject matter of conventional education is taught at an inappropriately early age. These lessons have been well assimilated in twentieth-century primary education, which advocates delaying the teaching of knowledge and skills until the child is 'ready'.

It is one thing, however, to recognize this as a sound and useful idea; it is another to portray it, as Rousseau does, as the centrepiece in one's philosophy. An acquaintance with ideas that one is incapable of grasping is liable to lead to misunderstanding, and Rousseau seems almost obsessed with the need to save people from this unfortunate condition. Hence his conception of 'negative education', the ideal approach with young children, which consists 'not in teaching virtue or truth, but in preserving the heart from vice and the mind from error' (p. 57, translation corrected).

There does seem to be an element of the irrational in Rousseau's hostility to falsehood. It is quite unreasonable, for example, to advance as a significant point that errors are more prevalent among learned Europeans than among primitive tribesmen. And his description of the mythical phoenix as one of the 'lies of antiquity' (p. 78) indicates a lack of sense of proportion. But despite some nonsense of this kind, Rousseau's main argument is a substantial one. We can best understand it by asking how it is that, if it is correct that children can only understand what they can experience, non-experiential curricula can operate with even a semblance of success. The explanation Rousseau gives is that children are clever at handling words: thus a question and answer session may seem to demonstrate that the teacher's lesson has been understood when in fact all that has been learned is how to answer the teacher's questions. Teachers therefore get a false impression of their achievements; but, most seriously of all, children come to equate learning with mere skill with words, giving them an exaggerated impression of how much they know.

Although there is a *prima facie* plausibility in Rousseau's claim that anything outside children's experience is meaningless to them, it has to be said that little argument is advanced for such a view: rather it is something that is indirectly supported by Rousseau's endorsement of the empiricist view of how anything can be known at all. Rousseau rigorously follows out the implications of this doctrine of the primacy of experience, almost *ad absurdum*. He complains, for example, about nurses who amuse their charges with words which are meaningless to children. Children should use only such words as they can understand. Since their understanding is limited, it is desirable that their vocabulary should be equally limited: so they should be kept from hearing any words that are beyond their understanding (pp. 37–40). Quite apart from the impractical nature of this advice, Rousseau's conviction that only experience can make words intelligible has surely led him into an implausible view of how language is acquired. To acquire language it is essential to hear words one does not understand. Words cannot be considered in isolation, for they acquire meaning from their context. We have to hear them in action, and then master their use by trying them out ourselves. Rousseau's idea is that learners must be familiar with the things signified before they can understand the signs. This is perhaps most plausible when the very young are mastering names like 'Mummy' and 'Teddy'. But even at this stage, not all words are labels: we know that toddlers all understand the word 'no', because they use it themselves as a monosyllabic expression of dissent. This kind of language use has to be borne in mind as at least an important qualification to Rousseau's account. At one level, this may be making too much of what, in *Emile*, is very much a passing point, but it does serve to underline that Rousseau's ideal does not involve children being reared within and initiated into an ongoing social life: he believes that children's development is best nurtured in a controlled environment specially selected or designed for educational purposes.

In *Emile*, experience and books are frequently contrasted as sources of knowledge for the young. Apart from the fact that books pass off mere verbalisms as real knowledge, reliance on books means, for Rousseau, reliance on other people's judgements. It is Rousseau's aversion to accepting any teaching on the basis of the teacher's authority which leads him to talk in terms of the centrality of reason. This is not to be taken as necessarily involving complex forms of thought, nor is it a challenge to the primacy of experience. It is Rousseau's way of stressing that we must all develop our own ideas, all try to make sense of the world for ourselves. The extent to which children can do this is, of course, limited; but Rousseau thinks we must just accept this. But more positively we can give children scope for judgement: one of Rousseau's criticisms of conventional education is that the system denies children any opportunity to reason, since it is not sufficiently free.

The positive pedagogic principle which arises from these considerations is usually called 'discovery learning'. Instead of being taught other people's ideas, Emile is to draw his own conclusions from his own experience. For one thing, the active use of one's mental powers in making sense of things gives one an increasingly resourceful mind. Hence Rousseau can say to the conventional educator: 'You teach science . . . I am busy fashioning the necessary tools for its acquisition' (p. 90).

As we have seen, negative education involves protection not just against error but against vice. How do these considerations bear on the child's moral development? In a state of nature children have no ideas of right and wrong. In society they unquestioningly accept the standards of those in authority. In a passage which appears to the twentieth-century reader totally Piagetian, Rousseau writes: 'until the age when reason becomes enlightened . . . what is wrong for young people is what those about them have decided to be wrong. What they are told to do is good; what they are forbidden to do is bad' (p. 344). For Rousseau, good and evil are knowable through reason: while reason is slow to develop, however, some moral learning can be had through experience.

The best-known example which Rousseau gives of this notion of experiential learning is of the pupil breaking his bedroom window only to find that it is left unrepaired: cold, draughty nights teach Emile not to behave like this (p. 64). This episode, however, seems to constitute a lesson in prudence rather than in morals. It should also be noted that the reactions of other people are included in the category of natural consequences from which Emile is to learn. For when Emile indulges in more widespread activities of this kind he finds that as a result he is locked in a windowless shed (a far cry from the kind of tactic one might expect from more fainthearted and sensitive progressives). In this predicament Emile hits upon the notion of a promise – a useful kind of contract which can satisfy the promisee and simultaneously extricate the promiser from a difficult situation.

It will be evident from this that although Emile is learning from experience, his experience is engineered by the tutor. One further episode will illustrate this. The tutor arranges for Emile to plant seeds in a piece of land which, it later transpires, has already been sown by the gardener. In the ensuing exchange with the gardener, Emile learns that there are some things over which people feel entitled to claim exclusive rights: thus Emile acquires the concept of property (p. 62 ff.). It is worth pointing out, however, that had Emile been reared in a family instead of in a state of isolation he would have learned this idea from his siblings in a way that was practical and memorable and which required no contrivance on the part of any adult. But the situation of the young Emile requires no sharing or co-operating and seems far from the kind of instructional setting which is conducive to moral education.

Rousseau cheerfully concedes this (and much else) in a review of Emile's development up to the age of fifteen (pp. 169–71). He has no under-standing of personal relationships, his imagination has not been devel-oped, and generally he has rather little knowledge: 'Emile's knowledge is confined to nature and things.' This means that he has some idea of mathematics, geography and science – the studies which arise from observation of the environment. He will also have learned a trade. On the credit side, 'what he knows is really his own; he has no half-knowl-edge'.

If this seems a dismally short checklist, this is a misunderstanding of Rousseau's strategy. Because reason develops late, he believes, education properly belongs to the post-fifteen stage (p. 173). Now the time has come when much learning can and should take place. Emile is to acquire an understanding of his fellow men not from real life (such lessons are corrupting or disillusioning) but from history books (p. 308). Emile may also study Greek, Latin and Italian poetry (p. 308). This suggests that we are given only a partial view of Rousseau when G. H. Bantock complains that Rousseau's writing depreciates the value of books (Bantock, 1965, p. 71). The main reason for turning to books at a late stage, after all, is that only then can books be used properly. In history books the formula which Rousseau (1762, p. 201) (rather optimistically) specifies is 'Facts! Facts! and let him decide for himself.' But younger children are not in a position to respond to the invitation to pass judgement. A further advantage in this delaying of bookish study is that unlike the conventional pupil who is book weary, Emile finds books novel and interesting at the very time when he can get most from them (*ibid.*, p. 280). And, like all child-centred educationists, Rousseau is very conscious of the potency of interest.

This chapter, properly or otherwise, has highlighted those principles in Rousseau's writing which are of lasting value. But in case Rousseau has been made to sound like a twentieth-century educationist, we must remember that he was writing in a very different period. And like anyone else, Rousseau must in some measure be understood as a man of his time. What were the significant characteristics of this period?

First, Rousseau himself saw it as an unstable period, with social upheaval looming. His writing shows a sensitivity to the fact that people to whom life has been kind are ill prepared for the possibility that their situations may change for the worse. At the beginning of *Emile* he writes: 'Those of us who can best endure the good and evil of life are the best educated' (*ibid.*, p. 9). And at the end he advises Emile: 'set yourself above the chances of life' (p. 410). To give everyone a reasonable chance of coping in reduced circumstances Rousseau believes that a trade should be learned as an integral part of one's education. In our own society, one of Scotland's most successful football managers has explained that at the beginning of each season he carefully checks his carpenter's tools in case he is removed from his post in the course of the year. Rousseau shares this sense of the precariousness of high-status positions, though of course it is the leisured aristocracy that he has in mind. Hence his desire to make carpenters of kings. The ability to support oneself through manual skills is an essential insurance against hard times; for though the currency of your aristocratic authority may lose its value, you can, as a skilled tradesman, still command an income that will provide the necessities without which, as we saw above, happiness is impossible. But as well as being safer, reliance on oneself is also more admirable than reliance on others. As so often, Rousseau makes the point in a way that is unforgettable: 'he who loses his crown and lives without it is more than a king; from the rank of a king . . . he rises to the rank of a man' (p. 157). Distinctions of rank are, in any case for Rousseau, 'artificial' – manmade deviations from a God-designed natural order.

By contrast with the fragility of the existing social order, where society is static children's futures can be seen as predictable. The son of a king, a lawyer, a baker or a farm labourer may effectively be destined to play roles similar to their fathers'. Consequently, their education is likely to be tailored to fit them for their pre-ordained stations in society; it is not so likely to be seen in terms of facilitating personal growth, or developing a resourceful mind. In fact Rousseau seems to have thought that only girls had a predictable future; their role was not just pre-ordained but also subordinate. This is why Rousseau thought it proper to devise for girls a quite different education, involving a curriculum which we would now see as both limited and limiting.

A second crucial characteristic of Rousseau's day involved the life expectancy of the newborn child. In the middle of the eighteenth century, only half the people born reached the age of fifteen, with the likelihood of dying at its greatest in the earliest years. The combination of swaddling and wet-nursing must inevitably have made a contribution to this: in between feeds, babies were sometimes strapped to a board and hung up on a peg! Given the religious framework within which most people thought, it is easy to see why infant mortality was generally accompanied by strict discipline. If there was a high risk of your own children departing prematurely to another world, you would want to ensure that their conduct and character were virtuous enough to ensure that they would be admitted to heaven. So the stern disciplinarian could also be seen as a caring parent.

Two other features of the time are worthy of note. One is the growth of science, testimony to what could be achieved by the unfettered intellect. Even though Rousseau had his reservations about the effects of this advance, it is very clear that it had a positive influence on his view of the ideal education (as indeed it continues to influence our view today). Emile is not to be swayed by beliefs which currently prevail in society and he is not to accept other people's conclusions. He is to be a person of independent judgement and enquiring mind, drawing his own conclusions on the basis of his observations of people and things.

Further, the advance of science and technology had brought new wealth and greater materialism to the growing cities – and in its wake, at least in the eyes of Rousseau the moralist, came a rampant immorality. In reacting against this, Rousseau was in the forefront of the romantic revival which reawakened interest in nature, generated an idealized picture of the countryside, and which saw in childhood a purity untainted by the corruption of the new age. First Blake and then Wordsworth were to celebrate childhood in such terms:

> not in utter nakedness
> But trailing clouds of glory do we come
> . . .
> Heaven lies around us in our infancy!
> (Wordsworth, *Intimations of Immortality*)

In all this there are perhaps two key insights for the late-twentieth-century educator. One is that children are slow to mature intellectually, and those responsible for their education should accept this. The second is Rousseau's emphasis on the importance of understanding, and his point that it is easy for teachers to be misled into thinking a child has understood something when no understanding has taken place.

These two points go well together. On a pre-Rousseau criterion, the good teacher might well be assumed to be the one who covers the greatest ground in the shortest time. But if the child's intellectual development is inescapably gradual, this approach is pointless: education has to proceed slowly. One slow way of learning – as its critics frequently point out – is discovery learning, or learning by experience. But in Rousseau's eyes this process of pupils having to think out their own conclusions is precisely the learning method which brings understanding. So there is no rational alternative to proceeding slowly. And even if one *could* educate quickly, it would be educationally advantageous to opt for a style of learning which is in fact gradual and laborious. The reasons for this are spelled out in a passage which concludes with one of Rousseau's many expressions of the perverse and the paradoxical.

> . . . the notions of things thus acquired for oneself are clearer and much more convincing than those acquired from the teaching of others; and not only is our reason not accustomed to slavish submission to authority, but we develop greater ingenuity in discovering relations, connecting ideas and inventing apparatus, than when we merely accept what is given us and allow our minds to be enfeebled . . . , we badly need someone to teach us the art of learning with difficulty.
>
> (Rousseau, 1762, p. 139)

In any case, methods of learning which appear to promote rapid development would conflict with one of the ground rules stated at the beginning of *Emile:* there must be agreement between the teacher's educational programme and nature's developmental programme (*ibid.*, p. 6). Since nature's programme – the rate at which children's faculties develop – is beyond our control, it must be the curriculum which is adapted to fit the child's rate of growth. There is no merit in trying to force the curricular pace. And since childhood is the 'sleep of reason', the curriculum must be experiential. This is still affirmed by child-centred education today, and it seems beyond dispute that the practical implementation of such insights has been of enormous benefit to children.

3

FOOTNOTES TO ROUSSEAU

If, as A. N. Whitehead suggested, the history of Western philosophy is a series of footnotes to Plato, then child-centred educational theory is a series of footnotes to Rousseau. This is not to be dismissive: some footnotes provide fully developed and important arguments. But for many writers the agenda and the tone were both clearly set by Rousseau: education needed to be redesigned along more rational lines to make it accord better with the nature of the learner.

It is possible to construct a line of succession through which Rousseau's message passed, with each thinker reworking the ideas of those who had written earlier. The key figures in this line are probably Pestalozzi and Froebel, Dewey and Kilpatrick; and it is hardly surprising to find that writers of such stature are discriminating in their adoption of progressive thinking. Far from merely echoing what was said before them, each of these subjected existing ideas to scrutiny and modification. Any criticism, however, was designed not to reject the basic position, but to ensure that this new approach to education was soundly based or wisely interpreted.

Pestalozzi was sixteen when *Emile* was published, and like many others then and now, he was intoxicated by Rousseau's writing. Under its influence Pestalozzi installed himself in a country cottage, experimented in farming, and called his only son Jean-Jacques. Later he took up teaching, eventually conducting his own school at Yverdon. In Pestalozzi's eyes, Rousseau snapped our mental chains, and became 'the turning point between the old world and the new in educational matters' (Pestalozzi, 1826, p. 319). Some of the central themes in Rousseau's account of learning and teaching were simply transposed into Pestalozzi's educational writings (which spanned a remarkable forty-five years).

Learning, he argued, should not proceed under duress because 'Man loses the equilibrium of his power, the strength of his wisdom, in proportion as his mind is compulsorily given up to the pursuit of an object. Hence the natural way of teaching is not coercive' (Green, 1912, p. 20)

Pestalozzi is here deploying Rousseau's distinction between the natural and the artificial; and he is endorsing Rousseau's view that traditional teaching produces only an outward show of learning: 'The artificial methods of the school which prefers the order of words to the free though slow sequence of Nature may make men superficially brilliant, hiding in this way their want of native power and satisfying times like ours' (*ibid.*, p. 19). Instead of dealing with words, the child should learn through activity and through things. He should be free to pursue his own interests and draw his own conclusions. He should not be made anxious or put under stress, and his development should not be forced.

> Parents should not hurry their children into working at things remote from their immediate interests. Let them first attain the strength that comes from dealing efficiently with matters near at hand. Be fearful of sternness and strain. By anticipating the ordinary course, they diminish the powers of their children, and disturb profoundly the equilibrium of their nature. This is what happens when teachers hurry children into lessons that are concerned chiefly with words, before they have passed through the discipline of actual encounter with real things. Yet it is out of such experience that wisdom and truth develop. The teacher's course lays the foundations of intellectual growth and power in empty words instead of in the solid truths that come from contact with realities.
>
> (*ibid.*, p. 19)

If the concept of 'solid truths' is a little quaint, the idea behind it is not. Any child-centred teacher now pursues a policy of providing 'contact with realities' in many different ways, believing that this is what provides a sound foundation for learning. Hence the importance attached to playing with bricks or with Lego, the use of Dienes' material for understanding arithmetical processes, or of paper-folding as a basis for understanding shape.

In *How Gertrude Teaches her Children* (1802) Pestalozzi saw his work as an attempt to 'psychologize' education, and he made explicit the need for the subject matter and the capacity of the learner to be matched or 'harmonized' – an idea which was to resurface much later in the Primary Memorandum and the Plowden Report: 'to instruct men is nothing more than to help human nature to develop in its own way, and the art of instruction depends primarily on harmonizing our message and the demands we make upon the child with his powers at the moment' (Green, 1912, p. 87).

For this to be achieved, however, two kinds of research would be required. The first necessity is 'a comprehensive and uninterrupted investigation of the ways and means employed by nature herself in the unfolding of our separate powers and of those higher laws by which she brings those separate powers into relation with the sum-total of all our faculties.' (*ibid.*) Further, as Pestalozzi explains in *Address to My House, 1818,*

> instruction in every branch of knowledge must be considered in relation to the fundamental faculties of human nature, and we must find out whether the devices and exercises in that particular study are in harmony with the natural development of those powers. We must also ascertain, in regard to every subject, what parts of it can be properly acquired by children – firstly through simple sensory activity, secondly through memory, and thirdly through imagination – and how such constituent parts can themselves be utilized on the one hand as a means of developing and exercising the fundamental natural faculties, and on the other hand simply as materials for acquiring knowledge of the subject, such as may be used later on when age and capacity permit.
>
> (*ibid.*, p. 208)

Here we begin to see that Pestalozzi goes beyond the mere reflection of Rousseau's ideas. He is not just expounding educational principles but sketching a possible way forward based on a programme of research. And this points to a feature of Pestalozzi's work which is a definite advance on anything to be found in *Emile*. Pestalozzi was committed to the education of all, rich and poor alike; and indeed he saw in education the key to the improvement of social conditions. But further, Pestalozzi gave some thought to how this could be implemented.

So there is in Pestalozzi just the kind of practical streak that might be expected from a schoolteacher. In *How Gertrude Teaches her Children* it is argued that before teaching a child reading and spelling, the child must have appropriate experience and a good vocabulary (*ibid.*, p. 87). To this end Pestalozzi developed picture books to provide the right kind of visual experience. Experience was seen as an equally crucial foundation for arithmetic:

> the beginnings of arithmetic should be taught through real objects, or through the use of dots representing them, if children are to be saved from future confusion and error . . . . If, for example, he [the teacher] asked in an arithmetic lesson, 'How many sevens are there in sixty-three?' the children had no intelligent background for their answers, and must carefully think them out. Now, under the new method, nine times seven objects are placed before him, and he learns to count nine groups of seven . . . . This is the type of procedure adopted in every subject.
>
> (*ibid.*, pp. 98–9)

Despite the importance attached to things, however, Pestalozzi's concern for the broad implementation of his 'method' led him to stress the value of suitable textbooks. Essentially these were thought of as the original 'teacher-proof' materials: for while Rousseau postulated a master-teacher who could devote himself to his pupil, Pestalozzi recognized that this was far removed from reality. Few teachers were experts and some teachers were ignorant. Yet Pestalozzi believed this need not matter (he even experimented with children teaching each other) provided they were equipped with well-designed textbooks. Again he argued that if these were to be soundly based, there would have to be research into

> the whole range of human knowledge, but giving special attention to points of departure in the process of development. In no other way can we insure a supply of school-books and textbooks suited to the actual situation. I saw, too, that the right solution of this book problem depended upon their careful graduation in accordance with the increasing capacities of children. We must also be in a position to say clearly and definitely what part of each subject is suited for each stage in the child's advance.
>
> (*ibid.*, p. 87)

But progress was also possible on another front. The Gertrude in the title of this work is a model mother; and Pestalozzi is keen to stress the learning potential of the social relationships of the home. Unfortunately 'one great evil of modern times which is a serious obstacle to progress is the fact that parents have lost the conviction that they themselves can do anything in the education of their children' (*ibid.*, p. 206). However, Pestalozzi has a suggestion for overcoming this difficulty as well. Educationists should produce a guidebook for parents that would explain what could and should be done.

> It would show them . . . how they might use the environment of the child, and employ systematic exercises in sensory apprehension to form, as it were, as a basis for the complete and more scientific studies of later life. In a like way it would lead parents to see how the thought powers and the practical powers of the children could be exercised and developed. In a word, the book would seek to show how the will, the knowledge, and the capacity, of the race would be 'naturally' helped on by simple means available in the poorest home.
>
> (*ibid.*, pp. 207—8)

Pestalozzi's school at Yverdon received many visitors. Two from Britain who were unimpressed were Robert Owen and Andrew Bell, the latter being one of the pioneers of the monitorial system of teaching which had no place for experiential learning. Bell later commented: 'I have now got to know your Pestalozzi's method. Believe me, in twelve years' time nobody will speak of it, while mine will have spread all over the earth' (Silber, 1973, p. 282). Happily Bell was wrong on both counts.

With insight we can see that Pestalozzi's most important visitor was Friedrich Froebel who spent two spells at Yverdon: on the first occasion, for a fortnight; on the second occasion, for two years. The original contact had been through a chance meeting between Froebel and one of Pestalozzi's former pupils.

Froebel admired much of what he saw: the nature walks, the games and songs, the conception of education as development, the attempt to base education on the nature of the child. Yet his observations on Pestalozzi were not uncritical: 'I knew the Pestalozzian method in its essential characteristics, but I did not see it as a living force such as would meet man's needs. I was oppressed by the fact that there was no organic connection between the subjects of instruction' (Lilley, 1967, p. 36). To twentieth-century minds this usage of 'empirical' and 'scientific' is strange. Froebel goes on to complain that in attempting to base education on human nature Pestalozzi was only concerned with man 'as existing . . . in his appearance on earth': it seems odd to see as more scientific his own approach which involved taking man 'in his eternal being'.

From this it will be clear that Froebel's thinking is based on theism. This provided the essential framework within which Froebel was able to discern 'unity' everywhere. This unity seems to embrace a wide range of relationships: between man and God, man and nature, 'mankind as a whole', and in the 'interconnection of all living things'. As well as offering a statement about how things are, unity also functions in Froebel's thinking as a goal. It was, for example, important to establish unity between one's inward and outward life. And in the criticism of Pestalozzi quoted above, it is clear that the curriculum should itself manifest unity.

This metaphysical outlook is closely related to Froebel's view of the nature of children and therefore to his preferred approach to education. 'Must we go on stamping our children like coins,' he asks, 'instead of seeing them walk among us as the images of God?' (Lilley, 1967, p. 156). If children are to be seen in this light, what kind of development should we be hoping for? In *The Education of Man* (1826) Froebel explains:

> Everything has a purpose, which is to realize its essence, the divine nature developing within it, and so to reveal God in the transitory world. Man has a special purpose. As a perceptive and rational being, he is intended to reach full awareness of his essential nature. He is meant to reveal the divine element within him by allowing it to become freely effective in his life.
>
> (Lilley, 1967, p. 49)

The divine element in human nature is the ability to be productive and creative, the model here being the Act of Creation. It is this that led Froebel to stress the importance of creating an educational environment that involved practical work and the handling of materials. This kind of school work was *not* advocated because of any limitations in the child's ability to grasp complex ideas without material aids. Practical work is said to be the way of nature and of God: it is the best way to achieve knowledge for adults as well as for children. '[Man] works primarily to give outward form to the divine spirit within him so that he may know his own nature and the nature of God' (*ibid.*, p. 65). Without this religious dimension, labourers would be mere beasts of burden. On Froebel's picture, however, they are blessed by their opportunities for daily toil: in fact Froebel supposes this to be Christ's reason for saying that the poor possess the kingdom of heaven. And he adds: 'So do children; if unchecked by adult presumption and folly, they will give themselves up to their innate desire for activity and creative work' (*ibid.*, p. 67).

Froebel notes that from the earliest stage, a child seeks to make shapes.

> But it is in painting and drawing in the strict sense, even if it is only drawing in the earth or on glass that he has breathed on, that attract him most of all. These are the most satisfying means of expression. . . .
> Yet so far drawing has not been generally regarded as essential.
>
> (*ibid.*, p. 115)

We have noted that active and creative work can be a means to knowledge. Froebel's picture of what is involved in the achievement of knowledge is itself different from ours. Ideas are not 'out there' waiting to be grasped by dint of intellectual effort. Instead we are born with potential awareness and understanding, and these become realized by a process of unfolding. Froebel seems so convinced that all development must consist of unfolding what is already there that this is used as an argument to demonstrate the necessity of innate understanding: 'Did it not lie in the child, did it not live and work in the child, did it not already define the child's life, it could by no means come out from it at a later period' (Froebel, 1840, p. 94).

Crucial to the development of the child's awareness is play. There is nothing lighthearted about Froebel's conception of play. He sees it as something important to the child, a type of occupation which is entered into purposefully. And in Froebel's own eyes, children's play is far from being just an agreeable diversion: it is an activity of great symbolic significance. As a form of creative activity, it is nothing less than a revelation of the divine in children. But it is also the means through which a child grows increasingly aware of the world and his place in it. This process is, or should be, a steady advance from the child's earliest impression of things as 'a vague, shapeless confusion into which he himself merges' (Lilley, 1967, p. 81). Unfortunately the education that is actually offered in the school or in the home often fails to provide the necessary scope for natural activity of the kind that will allow this awareness to unfold. Instead the young are provided with an artificial and inappropriate environment which Froebel claims, perhaps not very plausibly, either makes no impact, or too much impact on the child: 'we build a house of cards in which Nature finds no place and divine influence no room; it falls to the ground at the slightest touch of the child's real desires and impulses, but if it stands he is fettered in mind and body' (*ibid.*, p. 89). This failure on society's part to make adequate provision for the child's impulse to creative activity has serious consequences because the adult can reach maturity only if he has 'fulfilled the demands of childhood and adolescence' (*ibid.*, p. 64). In fact Froebel, like Rousseau, saw human development going through five stages: if one of these stages went past without the divinely implanted impulses and powers being translated into action, Froebel believed there could be no remedy.

Froebel's writing, like Rousseau's, is not short of the rhetoric of freedom. We are told, for example, that play should reflect 'the free activity of the whole life of the pupil's mind'. Such considerations are so important, however, that Froebel concludes

> Play . . . must not be left to chance. Just because he learns through play a child learns willingly and learns much. So play, like learning and activity, has its own definite period of time and it must not be left out of the elementary curriculum. The educator must not only guide the play, since it is so very important, but he must also often teach this sort of play in the first instance.
>
> (*ibid.*, p. 167)

Froebel's concern about the crucial function of play led him to devise a series of simple toys that would meet the child's developing needs and to which children should be introduced at appropriate stages of their development. These were called the 'gifts' – a series of shaped wooden bricks, some of which could be divided into segments; and the 'occupations' (little handwork sets). A detailed description of the equipment would not illuminate Froebel's thinking: what should concern us is *why* Froebel thought these things important. What is frequently missed or avoided in accounts of these playthings is that they are *symbolic*. The outcome of children's development is to be that they achieve an awareness of the unity of things. This awareness is of course present in the child in embryonic form. As an initial stimulus to prompt the unfolding of some awareness of this idea, the child is to be given a ball. The uninterrupted surface of a sphere makes it a symbol of unity. (The ring formation of participants in many children's games is also held to symbolize unity.) The sequence of gifts is meant to mirror and foster the child's developing awareness. In *Pedagogics of the Kindergarten* Froebel asserts

> It is important for him that he himself in play, even as a child, by play should perceive within and without how *from* UNITY *proceed* MANIFOLDNESS, *plurality, and totality*, and how *plurality and* MANIFOLDNESS *finally are found again in and resolve themselves into* UNITY, and should find this out in his life.
>
> (Froebel, 1840, p. 98, author's emphases)

Equally, some of the activities ('occupations') which Froebel recommended for children are not just what they seem. Sewing involves the experience of joining a series of points (the needle's pricks) into a line. Weaving is the conversion of lines into a flat surface.

Of course this equipment could be used in a much more mundane way as well. Froebel certainly seems to have been well enough aware of the potential of bricks for teaching numbers and fractions. But although he advises fathers not to answer questions, if it is possible, but instead to encourage children to work out answers for themselves, this does not seem to lead Froebel to advocate free play of the kind that we might today see infants engaged in with Lego bricks. Instead, five-year-olds are to be given directions which they have to follow:

> Lay four times two whole cubes in an oblong before you; place perpendicularly upon them again four times two whole cubes. Over each two cubes lay two half cubes, so that they touch in the middle by their sharp edges; with the last two cubes, each of the two half cubes yet required is represented by two quarters.

This was to be followed by a song:

> A house, a house, a house?
> A house belongs to me.
> A house, a house, a house?
> Come here, come here and see?
> In length it is four cubes,
> In breadth it is two cubes.

(Froebel, 1840, pp. 222–4)

Although the Plowden Report judged Froebel to have been the most influential of the progressive educational theorists, it is doubtful if much of this perceived influence can be related directly to his writing. Froebel's theory inspired a movement. Lectures and exhibitions were given in London in 1854; twenty years later the Froebel Society was formed; and in 1881 Froebel's grandniece set up a Pestalozzi-Froebel centre in Berlin. What seems most likely is that this movement familiarized the teaching profession with the idea that there was a role for play equipment in school. And the availability of equipment – something practical that teachers could use – probably commended Froebel's method to practitioners. But the use to which such equipment was subsequently put, however beneficial, was probably less heavy with significance than Froebel would have wished.

Undeniably, however, Froebel's name is well known to teachers today. Essentially it is associated with the education of *young* children, and perhaps the respectful treatment infants are given by teachers, and the scope they have for play are features of early education which do owe something to Froebel's thinking. Certainly the impressively supportive atmosphere of infant classrooms is a response to a widely recognized need long ago identified by Froebel: 'Children need encouragement as growing plants need warmth and light' (Lilley, 1967, p. 114). But by the middle of the twentieth century, a 'Froebel course' in a college of education was far removed from the philosophy of *The Education of Man*.

So far this review has been distinctly Eurocentric. While Pestalozzi's practice did cross the Atlantic, child-centred education was most influentially expounded and advocated in America in the philosophical writing of John Dewey. Of all writers of educational theory, probably Dewey has been more fully discussed than anyone. His impact in America on philosophy of education has been immense. What is also important is that Dewey helped to legitimate child-centred educational theory. As an established university teacher of philosophy he was able to develop his ideas in a way that gave them academic credibility.

Dewey shared Rousseau's admiration for simpler, rural societies. In such communities, Dewey thought, the environment was open to the understanding. Children could see sheep being sheared, wool being spun and cloth manufactured. They could understand the world of work and therefore the lives of their parents. But more than this, such an environment provided a vital moral education; for it was easy, natural, and sometimes essential, for children themselves to take part in these activities. The experience required for such learning was participation in community life; and 'community' was defined by Dewey in terms of shared purposes.

Unlike Rousseau, however, Dewey's thinking was strongly influenced by a further notion: social progress. So while there was much to admire in the simple, as well as much to deplore in the complex, it had to be recognized that social advances had been made. Some societies – and of course Dewey was thinking primarily of America – were more evolved than others, a concept borrowed from the newly influential thinking of Darwin. While most suppose that an undeveloped society is the natural consequence of a people with undeveloped minds, Dewey thought that limitations of the 'savage mind' were due to the limited environment it inhabited – there was simply no necessity to develop.

For any society, simple or developed, to survive, it has to ensure that children assimilate the ways in which we think and behave. In complex and sophisticated societies, the arrangements for learning are inevitably themselves complex and sophisticated. These arrangements are called schools, and Dewey accepts these where Rousseau rejected them.

Dewey's perspective on education thus has something of the social anthropologist in it. Education has a social function – either in helping it to survive by passing down the ways of the tribe, or in helping society to advance. There is, or ought to be, constant interaction between school and society, with influence being felt both ways. In our kind of society, it is not enough for schools simply to pass on an existing culture: they must help to formulate, consolidate and improve it, a process which Dewey described as the 'constant reweaving of the social fabric' (Dewey, 1916, p. 3). The implicit sense of social flux was of course very real in the America of that time since a continuous stream of immigrants brought the stimulus of variety of outlook and experience. In 1909, 70 per cent of New York children were of foreign-born parents (Cremin, 1961). Acceptance of flux goes along with and underlines the importance of community and the need for some degree of shared aims and values. This interest in community translates itself into Dewey's vision of classrooms in action where learning takes place through group activities – the running of shops, the cultivation of gardens, the staging of plays, or any other planned undertaking. In proceedings of this kind, teachers have a leadership role, but essentially they should share in the activities, with the distinction between teacher and learner being minimized. And in this approach lies the answer to the question of discipline: the activity imposes its own order. It is, argues Dewey, where the class is not a community that control requires the exercise of the teacher's will.

But this new model of classwork is also seen by Dewey as offering a rational strategy for learning. Learning and activity are, for Dewey, related in three vital ways. Becoming involved in projects brings the child to see the usefulness of understanding and information. Knowledge is brought to life in contexts where it is seen to be important. And the using of knowledge gives the pupil a firm grasp of it. We should, says Dewey, ensure that the learner engages in activities which 'clinch ideas – that is, perceived meanings or connections' (Dewey, 1916, p. 191). The traditional divorce of school learning and experience is bad for both: the learning process becomes sterile and is seen as irrelevant; activity outside school is not seen as something to be informed by intelligence and understanding. Good teaching, on the other hand, links up with out-of-school activities, interests and problems. However, what often happens is that teaching proceeds along traditional lines and creates artificial problems of its own. The overriding problem becomes one of how to please the teacher; and Dewey claims (anticipating the idea of what we now call the 'hidden curriculum') that this is what children unconsciously study rather than study the subject matter of the class (*ibid.*, p. 156).

Dewey's proposals contrast with what he calls 'the static cold-storage ideal of knowledge'. This view Dewey saw as endemic in schools which (he complained) tended to operate with predefined curricula, to treat everyone as though they were the same, and, above all, render learning passive. But it was not the curriculum that should be central, but the child. In characterizing this idea, Dewey gave child-centred education its own classic metaphor. In traditional education, he says,

> the centre of gravity is outside the child. It is in the teacher, the text-book, anywhere and everywhere you please except in the immediate instincts and activities of the child himself . . . . Now the change which is coming into our education is the shifting of the centre of gravity. It is a change, a revolution, not unlike that introduced by Copernicus when the astronomical center shifted from the earth to the sun. In this case the child becomes the sun about which the appliances of education revolve; he is the center about which they are organized.
>
> (Dewey, 1900, p. 51)

But while the child in such an equation was seen by Rousseau as an individual interacting with the *natural* environment, Dewey saw the child as essentially social. It was a mistake to hold – as Pestalozzi may have believed – that a child learns 'by merely having the qualities of things impressed upon him through the gateway of the senses' (Dewey, 1916, p. 29). The child learns through interacting with a *social* environment –

either an informal one like a family or, in the case of school, an institution specifically designed to foster learning. The progressively complex vocabulary which children need to acquire is, after all, itself a social phenomenon: words and concepts perform socially agreed functions. So, to take Dewey's own example, the meaning of the word 'hat' is learned through a shared activity – the putting on of hats to go out. Understanding is thus something acquired indirectly rather than as the result of direct instruction. Of the latter strategy, Dewey is scornful: 'It almost seems as if all we have to do to convey an idea into the mind of another is to convey a sound into his ear' (Dewey, 1916, p. 14). This is a classic instance of progressive lampooning of traditional practice: it is a caricature, but one that is not entirely unfair. The reader may well be reminded of science teachers who 'explain', say, osmosis by dictating notes on the subject.

For Dewey, then, the teacher was not an instructor of passive learners, nor a tester, nor a referee in a competition, nor an authority on particular subject matter – a teacher could hardly be expected to be expert in artwork and cookery and woodwork and drama and communications systems. The teacher's job was to arrange proceedings in such a way that learning is encouraged and made easier. On this model, the teacher becomes a co-planner of work, whose expertise is based less on academic knowledge – though a broad general knowledge will be necessary – than on an understanding of children and groups. Dewey looked forward to a time when psychology would be more developed, and would enable learning to be more expertly assisted. In particular, he saw psychology as unveiling the 'laws of growth' (Dewey, 1897).

For ultimately the business of education is to promote the growth of the individual. Again, however, education has to do its work indirectly, as a facilitating agency: so Dewey makes the point by saying that education has 'as its aim at every stage an added *capacity* of growth' (Dewey, 1916, p. 54, emphasis added). But here Dewey takes care to distinguish his own view from one that he attributes to Froebel in which the teacher draws out from the child what is required so that the child will ultimately match a predefined model.

Rousseau, Pestalozzi and Froebel were all religious: John Dewey was not. Freed from the constraints of a divine plan, Dewey's view of human development was conceived in terms of open-ended social interaction rather than as a quasi-mechanical unfolding process which he sees as involving a notion of complete and perfect unfoldedness. This goal Dewey described as 'transcendental': 'So far as experience is concerned it is empty; it represents a vague sentimental aspiration rather than anything which can be intelligently grasped and stated' (Dewey, 1916, p. 58). In any case there can be no completion of the development process because life, in Dewey's eyes, is itself a process of growth; the more growth, the better the life. But if growth is not peculiar to childhood, what is the rationale for schooling? 'The purpose of school education is to ensure the continuance of education by organizing the powers that ensure growth' (*ibid.*, p. 54). Given this view of lifelong growth, it makes no sense to draw a distinction between education and life, or to think of education as a preparation for life in society; rather education should be seen as itself a mode of social life. (It may be that pupils are in fact more inclined to see it in this light than are their educators.)

So while Dewey was at one with Rousseau and others in rejecting the traditional model of the passive learner in school, his distinctive contribution was his emphasis on *shared* activity – hardly an option open to the isolated Emile in his secluded rural setting. Whereas Emile was presented as learning through his contact with the physical environment, Dewey stressed the importance for children of human interaction.

> Where the school work consists simply in learning lessons, mutual assistance, instead of being the most natural form of co-operation and association, becomes a clandestine effort to relieve one's neighbour of his proper duties. Where active work is going on, all this is changed . . . . A spirit of free communication, of interchange of ideas, suggestions, results . . . becomes the dominating note.
>
> (Dewey, 1900, p. 29)

This co-operative and mutually helpful style of living and working was meant to continue into society as a whole: 'The teacher is engaged not simply in the training of individuals but in the formation of the proper social life' (Dewey, 1897, p. 439). For the purpose of characterizing Dewey's position, it has been useful here to make some comparison with *Emile*. But it will also be instructive to note Dewey's own observations on Rousseau. Dewey criticizes Rousseau on two counts. First, he maintains that Rousseau is foolish to advocate leaving the child's natural powers to develop spontaneously. In such an approach, Dewey objects, 'The constructive use of intelligence in foresight, and contriving, is . . . discounted; we are just to get out of the way and allow nature to do the work' (Dewey, 1916, p. 112). Secondly, he complains that Rousseau wants to take the child out of the environment, when he should be putting him into the kind of environment which will ensure fruitful growth. Dewey's own view is explained like this:

> The only way in which adults consciously control the kind of education which the immature get is by controlling the environment in which they act, and hence think and feel. We never educate directly, but indirectly by means of the environment. Whether we permit chance environments to do the work, or whether we design environments for the purpose makes a great difference.
>
> (Dewey, 1916, pp. 18–19)

What is striking about Dewey's criticisms of Rousseau is that they are both completely misplaced. Emile's tutor frequently intervenes in his pupil's development. As we have seen, pedagogical power is deployed so discreetly that Emile is unaware that many of his apparently chance experiences are in fact engineered by his manipulative mentor. The strategy which Rousseau commends for the effective exercise of control is one of subtle deception.

Further, Emile is not to be educated 'apart from the environment' as Dewey suggests (Dewey, 1916, p. 118). Rather Emile is to be protected from the ethos of a sophisticated society which Rousseau sees as irredeemably pernicious. He is to spend his formative years in a simpler environment which is judged conducive to the kind of development which is appropriate and desirable for a child. One of the merits which Rousseau sees in this rural environment is that here it is possible for the tutor to control the kind of influence to which Emile is exposed. 'While the child is still unconscious there is time to prepare his surroundings, so that nothing shall strike his eye but what is fit for his sight . . . . You will not be master of the child if you cannot control everyone about him' (Rousseau, 1762, p. 59). Although Rousseau is both more thoroughgoing and less open, he is in principle at one with Dewey in thinking that the teacher should select the influences to which the pupil is exposed.

Dewey's thinking was continued through the work of his disciple William Kilpatrick who was a professor at Teachers College, Columbia, for twenty years. Lawrence Cremin explains:

> Teachers College was training a substantial percentage of the articulate leaders of American education. Any competent teacher occupying the senior chair of philosophy of education at the College between 1918 and 1938 would have exerted a prodigious influence on educational theory and practice. In the hands of the dedicated, compelling Kilpatrick, the chair became an extraordinarily strategic rostrum for the dissemination of a particular version of progressive education
>
> (Cremin, 1961, p. 220)

The essence of that version lies perhaps in Kilpatrick's emphasis on interest and motivation. This is outlined in his well-known paper 'The project method', published in the *Teachers College Record*. Here he takes up Dewey's theme of the ideal school as a 'regime of purposeful activity'. From tasks that are willingly entered into, we could, according to Kilpatrick, expect a child to derive

(i)   a high degree of skill and understanding
(ii)   knowledge that will be permanent
(iii) pleasure in his school work
(iv) enthusiasm for further projects
(v)   more favourable attitudes to social agencies generally.

> (Kilpatrick, 1918, pp. 326–7)

Kilpatrick hoped that the result of his favoured approach to schooling would be 'better citizens, alert, able to think and act, too intelligently critical to be easily hoodwinked either by politicians or by patent-medicines, self-reliant, ready of adaptation to the new social conditions that impend' (*ibid.*, p. 334). The values revealed in these two quotations are exactly what one would expect from progressive education.

Where Kilpatrick was arguably introducing something new was in the standards of clarity, exactness, and plain speaking that he wanted to see in progressive educational theory. This is certainly what emerges from his book, *Froebel's Kindergarten Principles Critically Examined* (1916). Kilpatrick credits Froebel with being instrumental in bringing play and practical work into the classroom. But he objects to kindergarten play being generally used as 'the means of presenting in symbolic form to early childhood certain quasi-metaphysical ideas' (Kilpatrick, 1916, p. 102). And he criticizes Froebel's use of the sphere as 'baseless symbolism' (*ibid.*, p. 79).

Kilpatrick's assessment technique consists of assembling from different parts of Froebel's writing various utterances on a particular theme, and viewing these as discrete statements removed from the charged contexts in which they originally emerged. The reader is asked to consider dispassionately whether these claims bear examination. For example, the following observations made by Froebel about the number five are laid out for critical inspection:

> truly the number of analytic and synthetic life, representing reason, unceasing self-development, self-elevation . . . unmistakable evidence of a higher phase of life . . . all kernel and stone-fruit trees . . . express the number five in their blossoms, as though the special enjoyableness of these fruits lay in their law of the number five running through them.
>
> (*ibid.*, p. 37)

And Kilpatrick observes

> to portray the significance of this number, in the Mother Play book a picture is given to the family of the five fingers, in which one wearies counting the number of fives: five people, five deer, five rabbits, etc, etc. Certainly twenty-five separate groups of five appear in this one picture. When it is recalled that the orthodox conservative kindergartner believes that these symbolic pictures have their pedagogic effect, the limit of mystic credulity seems surely found.
>
> (*ibid.*, p. 37)

One might reasonably question the practice of searching out the daftest pronouncements of any educationist. To the charge that Kilpatrick may risk discrediting some of Froebel's more valuable ideas, he might well reply that it is Froebel himself who undermines the case for play by arguing it in a metaphysical setting. ('Mystical' and 'metaphysical' are terms of disapprobation for Kilpatrick, as 'transcendental' is for Dewey.) And it has to be borne in mind that if writers' claims are never to be scrutinized, then there is no effective limit on what they can say. In addition to this kind of examination, which verges on plain ridicule, Kilpatrick employs another cutting implement: his demand for consistency. For example, he alleges that 'development' has a shifting meaning in Froebel's writing (Kilpatrick, 1916, p. 91), and that while Froebel demands maximum freedom for the child he also maintains the need for close and constant guidance (*ibid.*, p. 80).

In his application of these dogged checks to Froebel's writing, Kilpatrick seems to be anticipating the style of the philosophy of education which emerged in the 1960s, and which will be examined later in this book. The crucial difference is the degree of agreement to be found between the critic and the subject of the critique: in Kilpatrick there is at least an element of respect for the practical thrust of Froebel's writing if not for its tone or mode of argument. In this forerunner of contemporary philosophy of education, criticism is being made from within the progressive tradition, and this makes a difference.

4

GATHERING SUPPORT

Dewey's influence was massive. His thinking fed directly into many American schools, particularly in Chicago where one of Dewey's associates eventually became superintendent of schools. In the early years of the revolution, the Soviet Union seems to have been as enthusiastic about the 'project method' as it was about Dewey's stress on community and his strictures on élitism. Chinese students studying in the United States took Dewey's ideas back to China with them when they returned (Passow, 1982). And Dewey himself lectured in China. In Britain, however, the educational mainstream seems to have been less open to new ideas. As has been remarked elsewhere about educational theory, 'The European intellect has often had a difficult Channel crossing' (Coveney, 1967, p. 280). Early in the twentieth century, however, a group of educationists emerged which was to play a crucial role in putting schools in touch with the new educational ideas which had been developed in other countries.

Between the wars the outstanding champion of child-centred approaches to education was the New Education Fellowship (NEF), which brought together all those who were critical of traditional ways. The organization grew out of the Theosophical Educational Trust which founded several small, independent progressive schools.

Two prominent theosophist educationists were particularly important. One was Edmond Holmes, author of *What Is and What Might Be* (1911), who had been an inspector of elementary schools before becoming interested in Eastern religion. His book compares the traditional approach to schooling unfavourably with an actual progressive school admired by the ex-inspector. This denunciation of the system was, of course, all the more potent for coming from one of its own experienced officials. The other significant theosophist was Beatrice Ensor who founded the educational journal *The New Era*, and whose influence over the NEF was both long lasting and all pervading.

For diplomatic reasons, however, the NEF and Beatrice Ensor played down the Fellowship's original indebtedness to theosophy – a religious movement with a strange history and limited appeal. For the NEF was intended to be not just a meeting place for the enlightened but a missionary band for spreading the good news. Its deliberations have been criticized as being short on rigour and as exuding 'vague principles' (Selleck, 1972, p. 46). This was probably an inevitable weakness given that one of its roles was to give support to a wide range of individuals all with their own visions of child-centred education. With this diversity of viewpoints, the less closely the philosophy was examined, the less danger of dissension. Perhaps the Eastern ideals of harmony and serenity exercised excessive influence. The word 'new' in the organisation's name, of course, is not intended to indicate that it was a new fellowship: it was a fellowship for the promotion of 'the new education', a term then widely used (by Dewey among others) to refer to educational progressivism and the child-centred approach. The new education was seen in terms of revolutionary change away from a type of education which was outmoded in a modern age.

Within the NEF much of the interest was focused on innovative work in schools. In Britain this was characteristically, though not exclusively, to be found in small, private, pioneer establishments, often boarding schools, caustically labelled by A. S. Neill as 'crank' schools (a category which apparently excluded his own libertarian boarding school, Summerhill). These schools were so varied in character that none of them can be said to be typical of the genre. Yet some indication may be legitimately given about the kind of ideas that were abroad in this group by looking at a particular example.

The Forest School in Hampshire provides a good illustration of the pioneering spirit and the sheer idiosyncrasy that often characterized these ventures. This school was founded by a Quaker and run by the Order of Woodcraft Chivalry – a distant relative of the scouting movement. It was situated in a wood and prominence was given to the study of nature. In addition to conventional elements of the curriculum like arithmetic, credit was given to children for skills like canoeing and tree-climbing. Its first prospectus stated: 'At the Forest School the child is brought into touch with realities and is helped by a practical pursuit of the primitive arts to realise that he can learn by doing' (van der Eyken and Turner, 1969, p. 138).

Perhaps the key point, however, is that the school deliberately cut itself off from society, rejected society's values, and set up its own little society with its own values and way of life. One of the teachers describes the proceedings as follows:

The Order of Woodcraft Chivalry, discarding fossilised ritual, but realising that human beings need colour, had devised ritual of their own. For their meetings they wore strange druidical costumes. They rebaptised themselves with Red-Indian names like Great Bear, Rising Sun, Laughing Water, Otter and Golden Eagle . . . . When members met one another they raised their arms and uttered the greeting 'Blue Sky'. . . .

One Sunday every month there was a ritual meeting . . . . The President said 'Let the Keeper of the Fire light the fire!' The Keeper stepped forward and there was silence as the glow spread into enveloping flames. Then the Keeper cried: 'Behold the fire! It leaps, it glows, it burns! So may the Great Spirit leap and glow and burn within you.'

(Mackenzie, 1970, p. 9)

Two points can usefully be taken from this climax to the ritual. First, the Keeper's message embodies the kind of emotional aspiration to higher things which runs through this part of the progressive movement. Second, the sentiment is ill defined: what spirit, and to what effect is it to burn? This perhaps reinforces the claim that only by avoiding rigorous definition could such a diverse group of schools and educationists see each other as allies. Maurice Punch (1973, p. 4) alleges that the progressive educational ideology 'never approximated to a readily identifiable doctrine but was more a philosophical flag of convenience that tenuously united a diverse group of thinkers and practitioners'.

If the NEF was short on philosophical rigour, however, it lacked nothing in evangelical fervour. Its central proselytizing strategy was to stage conferences both local and international. The sense of enlightenment advancing on an international front was doubtless intoxicating, even though progressive thinking in some of the countries represented was probably confined to a mere handful of people. It may be that this determination to let ideas flow from one country to another owed something to the internationalist basis of theosophy. In India, where theosophy had been founded, there was a section of the NEF run by Radhakrishnan and Rabindranath Tagore. From across the Atlantic, members of the Progressive Education Association attended early NEF conferences in Montreux (1923) and in Scotland (1925). Some years after Dewey became president of the Progressive Education Association (the PEA), it became the American section of the NEF, and it spent the last years of its existence under the title of the American Education Fellowship (Cremin, 1961, p. 248).

The thinking underlying the NEF's internationalism was described at the Nice Conference in 1932:

The New Education Fellowship is organized on a world basis, and that is profoundly significant. It is perhaps inevitable from the nature of things that Education be organized on national lines. But an education which stops at nationalism is not realizing its true function. It is the business of education to make good Englishmen, good Frenchmen, good Germans, but above all good citizens of the world. We are learning that nationalism, simple nationalism and nothing more, is perhaps the most dangerous and explosive force in the world today.

(Rawson, 1933, p. 168)

Admittedly the reference in this argument to the English, the French and the Germans makes the argument look like a very Eurocentric version of internationalism. And although there were participants at this conference from fifty-three countries, the names of some of the speakers tend to confirm this impression: Northern Rhodesia was represented by Audrey Richards, Tanganyika by S. Rivers-Smith, and Nigeria by Lord Lugard. Jean Piaget argued at this conference that to change from nationalistic thinking to internationalistic thinking would be a move comparable to the way a child is freed 'from the intellectual and moral self-centredness of childhood': the teacher must help the child to create the required new intellectual tool and moral attitude (Rawson, 1933, pp. 15–16).

Inspection of NEF reports serves to reveal some of the other ideas advanced at these conferences. The first was held in 1921 in Calais, described by A. S. Neill as 'the ugliest town on earth – I hope' (Croall, 1983, p. 114), its main theme declared to be 'The creative self-expression of the child'. Neill gave a lecture advocating the abolition of authority and moral teaching. NEF chroniclers of the event rather coyly observed: 'For a good many of those present, and especially for continental people who had not had the chance to learn from the *Dominie* books how much wisdom lay behind the occasional extravagance, this appeared dangerous doctrine' (Boyd and Rawson, 1965, p. 72).

Perhaps the most important outcome of this gathering was the formulation of NEF principles. These speak of the need 'to respect the child's individuality' and 'to give free play to the child's innate interests'. Here we recognize some of the unshakable axioms of child-centred thinking. Other ideas referring to children's spiritual energy and spiritual power seem to have lasted less well.

After Calais the NEF convened international gatherings every second year, and by 1929 could command an audience of 1,800 delegates. In Denmark that year there were lectures from Maria Montessori, from Harold Rugg (a professor at Teachers College and co-author of *The Child-Centred School*) and from Scotland's William Boyd, who had earlier written: '*Emile* was by far the most considerable book written on education in the eighteenth century: judged by effects on thought and action, indeed, perhaps the most considerable book ever written on education' (Boyd, 1921, p. 301).

The theme of this conference was 'The new psychology and The curriculum'. In keeping with the sentiment embodied in the theme of the first conference, there was considerable interest in art education. A professor from Vienna declared:

If anything really interests children, they can give it form. The facts
they learn in school are graved in their minds by outward expression,
and they themselves are doubly enriched. They have added a few
more coloured pieces to the mosaic of their life. So considered, art
education is the heart of the whole educational system.

(Boyd, 1930, p. 227)

The time devoted by the conference to art in the curriculum reflected this
view, and the conference featured exhibitions of children's art from
different countries.

The fundamental concern with the nature of the child was further
developed at an NEF conference in New Zealand in 1938. With 5,000
teachers enrolled at different centres, and audiences overflowing from
halls with a capacity of 3,000, this was the climax of the Fellowship's
crusade. At this conference, Susan Isaacs declared: 'The child between 7
and 11 is a lively and vital person, active, curious, eager to achieve real
knowledge . . . . His interests are concrete – in persons and things rather
than in ideas' (Campbell, 1938, pp. 287–8). In another lecture she made a
claim which was seen not just as applicable to everyone within a primary-
school age range but as relevant equally to the adolescent and the infant:

The 'principle of activity' expresses the empirically discovered truth
that the child grows by his own efforts and his own real experience,
whether it be in skill or knowledge, in social feeling or spiritual
awareness. It is not what we do to the child or for the child that
educates him, but what we enable him to do for himself, to see and
learn and feel and understand for himself, and this is equally true of
the young infant, the school child and the adolescent.

(Campbell, 1938, p. 83)

It has been suggested in this chapter that the New Education Fellowship
played a crucial part in the development of child-centred education. On
the face of it, it may seem unlikely that the practice of progressive teaching
in small independent schools could be seen as offering a convincing
demonstration which might serve as a model. After all, the circumstances
of the progressive independent school are peculiarly advantageous: the
staff–pupil ratio is favourable; the pupils often come from prosperous and
accomplished family backgrounds; and the parents through their choice of
school have indicated their support for its distinctive philosophy. Clearly
it would be simple-minded to assume that successful practice in a school of
this kind could be directly transplanted into an average school. Instead
one has to look for influence of a less direct kind. While Summerhill
School, for example, had few imitators, Neill's well-publicized practice of
allowing children to absent themselves from all classes clearly stimulated
reconsideration of previously unquestioned assumptions. In general, the
mere existence of these schools kept the educational world alive to the fact
that alternative approaches to education are conceivable.

One example of indirect impact can be found in the Forest School. The
teacher whose account of this school has been quoted earlier in the chapter

went on to be an influential headteacher in the Scottish state system. Another illustration of this kind of influence is the case of Susan Isaacs who ran the experimental Malting House School for the first four years of its brief existence. Her ideas spread not directly through her work at the school but through two books on child development which she wrote after she left, and through her teaching when she became head of the department of child development at London University's Institute of Education. This department saw itself as producing lecturers for training colleges (Taylor, 1990, p. 246), a role which, as we shall see, the Institute was later to play in philosophy of education.

It has also been suggested that the New Zealand lectures represent the NEF's crusade at its peak. This evangelical metaphor is to be found in the foreword contributed by the New Zealand minister of education to the report of the proceedings: 'The Conference resulted in an educational revival . . . It has aroused and revivified interest in education in all parts of the country. Some of us hope, and have good grounds for believing, that it marked the commencement of an educational renaissance from which much will come' What came, however, was the Second World War, and after the war the NEF in Britain failed to re-emerge with the same vigour.

Three possible reasons could be advanced for this relative decline. Much of the impetus for this kind of educational work in the 1920s had arisen from a desire to rebuild society along more intelligent, enlightened, internationalist lines so that the horrors of the First World War would not be repeated. A second European war must have been crushingly disheartening and disillusioning.

Secondly, the post-war period saw the emergence of working-class power. This was something quite alien to many of the people involved in the NEF (Boyd being a notable exception here). Although Ramsay Macdonald and the TUC had both shown interest in their work, the NEF had built their thinking on the select and sometimes precious circles which patronized non-conforming private schools, and they had little knowledge of the social and economic realities of family poverty and the world of low-paid work. To the post-war bearers of the red flag, the NEF must have looked incredibly naive. While the Fellowship planned for a new era, its members belonged to an old one.

Finally the NEF may have declined because they had done a good job: the best evangelists always put themselves out of business. Perhaps we had not yet reached the stage forecast by Dewey when progressive education would mean the same as good education. Nevertheless, the persuasiveness of the child-centred case had been felt in influential places: the demerits of traditional teaching no longer needed to be argued.

An important part of the evidence for this is the 1931 Hadow Report on Primary Education (Consultative Committee, Board of Education, 1931), a significant forerunner of the official endorsements of child-centred education which were published in the 1960s. Its approach to primary education frequently echoes the early progressive theorists: oral evidence had been given to the committee by the NEF.

According to Hadow, the guiding idea for a good primary school

> must above all be the requirements of its pupils during the years when they are in its charge, not the exigencies of examinations or the demands of the schools and occupations which they will eventually enter. It will best serve their future by a single-minded devotion to their needs in the present, and the question which most concerns it is not what children should be – a point on which unanimity has hardly yet, perhaps, been reached – but what, in actual fact, children are. Its primary aim must be to aid children, while they are children, to be healthy and, so far as is possible, happy children, vigorous in body and lively in mind.
>
> (*ibid.*, p. xvi)

Here we must note the rejection of long-term goals for education. This is not to say that schools do not have long-term benefits. Instead it involves the belief that the best way of realizing these is not to identify an ideal future condition and then deduce what kind of schooling is required: one should rather attend to the enrichment of the child's present life and be assured that long-term benefits will follow. This view appears to have the convenient consequence for the theoretician that value-laden goals can be avoided: what is required is a knowledge of what children are. The implication is that primary education ought to be built on a study of the nature and development of children – a view which characterizes progressivism from Rousseau right up to the present day. The only aim which the report allows itself is one – health, happiness and vigour – to be enjoyed in childhood rather than projected into adulthood.

There may be an inconsistency here. We have after all been told by Hadow that 'the question which most concerns [the primary school] is not what children should be'. Yet these stated goals in fact constitute clues which serve to identify the kind of development that we should be hoping to see. The job of the primary educator then becomes the provision of whatever nourishment is needed to promote this kind of growth; and what is needed, so it is suggested, will depend on the child's stage of development.

> In framing the curriculum for the primary school . . . our main care must be to supply children between the ages of seven and eleven with what is essential to their healthy growth – physical, intellectual and moral – during that particular stage of their development. The principle which is here implied will be challenged by no one who has grasped the idea that life is a process of growth in which there are successive stages, each with its own specific character and needs.
>
> (*ibid.*, p. 92)

Arguments of this kind will be critically reviewed in Chapter 7.

The idea that life is a process of growth is one of the ideas in the Hadow Report that appears to be taken directly from Dewey. The report also cites

Dewey when explaining why we now need to think of the primary school as promoting not just good learning but good living as well.

> in the earliest days of popular education children went to school to learn specific things that could not well be taught at home – reading, writing and cyphering. The real business of life was picked up by a child in unregulated play, in casual intercourse with contemporaries and elders, and by a gradual apprenticeship to the discipline of the house, the farm, the workshop. But as industrialisation has transformed the bases of social life . . . discipline associated with the old forms of industrial training has become increasingly difficult outside the walls of the school. The schools whose first intention was to teach children how to read have thus been compelled to broaden their aims until it might now be said that they have to teach children how to live.
>
> *(ibid.,* p. 92)

Conditions in the years of the Depression were hardly ideal for implementing the Hadow approach to primary education. Who could afford to take no thought for tomorrow? In such difficult times, who was going to be impressed by a document which advised against paying too much attention to the requirements of the world of work? If the effect of Hadow on schools must necessarily have been limited, however, at the level of educational thought these ideas had clearly made their mark. And for many, a single authoritative pronouncement in an official report would be more persuasive than a hundred declarations from speakers at NEF conferences.

One way or another, the seed had been well sown. If conditions did not yet allow it to sprout, progressive thinking certainly seems to have germinated. Particularly fertile soil was provided by those key institutions, the teachers' training colleges. By the end of the war, teacher trainers had largely been persuaded of the merits of the child-centred approach to education. A college principal explains the prevailing view:

> ideas current in training institutions at the time . . . are usually described as progressive education, but although its advocates in the state system knew of the private progressive schools such as Summerhill or the Malting House School, practice in the colleges owed more to the Hadow Reports of 1931 and 1933, with their emphasis on 'activity' and 'experience'. It also had its roots in Froebelianism, particularly in its belief in the importance of play as the foundation of learning. The potential of children in the ordinary schools was to be fostered by allowing them more freedom for individual development, including artistic development, than they had hitherto experienced.
>
> (Browne, 1987, p. 88)

In the 1960s teacher training was expanding for two kinds of reasons. First, the school service itself was growing: there were more children to be schooled, and there was also a demand for smaller classes. So more new teachers were going into schools than previously. The child-centred philosophy tended to be favoured by teachers who were younger or more recently trained (see Chapter 5): so schools were increasingly staffed by teachers who were well disposed to this kind of thinking.

Secondly, in England the period of non-graduate training was extended to three years at the start of the decade. Between 1960 and 1970 the numbers of college staff increased more than threefold (Simon, 1983) and figures for teachers-in-training more than doubled (Bruce, 1985). In Scotland the demand for teachers necessitated the building of three new colleges of education (two of which have since been closed again). Where new college lecturers were being recruited in the child-centred climate of the 1960s, the progressive orientation noted by Browne is likely to have been even more marked. With a surge of newcomers into the profession, the position of gatekeeper became one of the most significant in the educational system: in college lecturers, child-centred education acquired some crucially important friends.

5

CHILD-CENTRED
EDUCATION ARRIVES

What finally confirmed the colleges in their view of the best approach to
primary education was the appearance in the 1960s of England's Plowden
Report and Scotland's Primary Memorandum. Of course college staff had
been included on the relevant committees and thus had themselves some
small say in the deliberations. But the publication of these reports gave
stature to the new pedagogy in a way that college teachers could never
have done on their own. The Primary Memorandum (SED, 1965) and the
Plowden Report (CACE, 1967) were landmarks in the development of
child-centred education in Britain. *Primary Education in Scotland* (the
Primary Memorandum) was written by a committee of inspectors, college
lecturers and headteachers. *Children and their Primary Schools* (the
Plowden Report) was the work of the Central Advisory Council for
Education, a group which included an educational psychologist, a
professor of 'child health and growth', and the principal of the Froebel
Institute College of Education. Interestingly, while the Primary Memorandum makes no reference to Hadow, the Plowden Report makes no
reference to the Primary Memorandum. Each proceeds as though thinking in its own country developed in isolation from the other: inspection of
some of the basic themes in each, however, reveals a remarkable degree of
harmony.

In its preface, the Primary Memorandum speaks approvingly of 'The
growing acceptance by teachers of the principles underlying an education
based on the needs and interests of the child and the nature of the world in
which he is growing up. Through a wide range of experiences the pupil is
given opportunities to participate actively in his learning' (SED, 1965, p.

vii). The reader is informed that the proposals put forward in the Primary Memorandum 'are based on what is known of the growth and development of the child, and emphasis is laid on the importance of fashioning the curriculum according to his needs at the various stages of his development' (*ibid.*, p. viii). To underline the importance of the point, the same position is restated at the beginning of the first chapter: 'The pattern of education in the primary school years must . . . above all have regard for the nature of the child and for the way he grows and develops during this period' (p. 3). This is exactly the philosophy of the Hadow Report; if there is a difference, it is in the manner of stating it. In the Primary Memorandum there is less emphasis on the rejection of a non-progressive outlook; quite simply there was less need for this. As the Memorandum put it, 'It is *now generally accepted* that the primary school is much more than a preparation for the secondary school: it is a stage of development in its own right' (p. 3, emphasis added).

From these broad statements of underlying principles, we now turn to the implications for teaching. First, allowance must always be made for the fact that a class consists of a collection of individuals who are not all the same: in particular, cognisance must be taken of their varying learning speeds.

> It is vital that these individual differences should be recognised and catered for in all spheres of the child's activities in school. The teacher's methods and organisation should be sufficiently flexible to allow each child to progress at an appropriate pace, and to achieve satisfaction and success at his own level.
>
> (*ibid.*, p. 4)

The flexibility demanded here may refer to the teacher's ability to deploy, as appropriate, individual methods, group methods and whole-class methods. In practice, however, the Memorandum goes out of its way to stress the advantages of a group-based class organization for learning and teaching. Groups can be either ability based or interest based, and will apparently 'emerge'.

> the benefits that derive from group methods entirely justify the effort. Many teachers have proved that in the permissive yet controlled atmosphere of the classroom where there is a flexible organisation and group methods skilfully employed, the able pupils can realize their potential, and all can achieve success at appropriate levels. In addition, self-reliance and initiative are developed, and the pupils have opportunities of pursuing individual enthusiasms, and of learning to share in co-operative enterprises.
>
> (*ibid.*, p. 68)

Second, while the importance of basic skills and knowledge is recognized, even more importance is attached to the cultivation in children of desirable attitudes to learning: 'Factual knowledge in itself is of less importance than the urge to ask questions, and the will and ability to find answers' (p. 18). Third, the Memorandum stresses an approach to learning which involves activity, experience and discovery: 'It is now recognised that learning occurs most effectively when the learner is personally involved in purposeful activity which captures his interest or arises from it. Consequently the emphasis in primary education is now more on learning by the pupil than on instruction by the teacher' (p. 60). Now less involved in instruction, the teacher will, 'to a greater extent than hitherto, encourage the child to do as much as possible for himself, in the knowledge that the more he learns through his own experiences and discoveries, the more meaningful and the more lasting his learning is likely to be' (p. 60). The design of the curriculum itself is to be reconceptualized along non-traditional lines:

> the curriculum is not to be thought of as a number of discrete subjects, each requiring a specific allocation of time each week or each month. Indeed, it is quite impossible to treat the subjects of the curriculum in isolation from one another if education is to be meaningful to the child.
>
> (*ibid.*, p. 37)

Finally, primary education is now to be understood as transcending the curriculum: 'It cannot be too strongly stressed that education is concerned as much with the personal development of the child as with the teaching of subjects' (p. 37).

Much of the Memorandum's thinking anticipated what was subsequently to appear in the Plowden Report. Plowden is equally sensitive to the felt needs and expressed interests of the child:

> The intense interest shown by young children in the world about them, their powers of concentration on whatever is occupying their attention, observing their immediate purposes, are apparent to both teachers and parents. Skills of reading and writing or the techniques used in art and craft can best be taught when the need for them is evident to children . . . . There is, therefore, good reason for allowing young children to choose within a carefully prepared environment in which choices and interest are supported by their teachers.
>
> (CACE, 1967, p. 195)

The Plowden Report sees much benefit to be had from the study of the ways in which children grow: 'Knowledge of the manner in which children develop . . . is of prime importance, both in avoiding educationally harmful practices and in introducing effective ones' (*ibid.*, p. 7). Like the Memorandum (and the Hadow Report before it), the Plowden Report endorses an approach to primary education which focuses on children as they are rather than on some long-distance end-product. A 'general and quickening trend' is observed where the school becomes 'a community in which children learn to live first and foremost as children and not as future adults' (p. 187). Notice here the implicit breadth of aim which is also to be found in both the Memorandum and in Hadow: schools are places where children learn to live. But it seems that learning to live entails not so much conforming to the requirements of others as the development of potential in an individualistic manner: 'In family life children learn to live with people of all ages. The school sets out deliberately to devise the right environment for children, to allow them to be themselves and to develop in the way and at the pace appropriate to them' (p. 187). Teaching too is to become individualized: 'Individual differences between children of the same age are so great that any class, however homogeneous it seems, must always be treated as a body of children needing individual and different attention' (p. 25).

As in the Primary Memorandum, this point is seen as perfectly compatible with, or perhaps even to require, group methods in the classroom. According to Plowden, group work is natural; it encourages children to assist each other; and it provides opportunities for discussing and planning joint enquiries. Once again, knowledge is said to be best acquired through activity and experience; and the importance of fostering good attitudes to learning is stressed.

> . . . activity and experience, both physical and mental, are often the best means of gaining knowledge and acquiring facts. This is more generally recognised today but still needs to be said. We certainly would not wish to undervalue knowledge and facts, but facts are best retained when they are used and understood, when right attitudes to learning are created, when children learn to learn. Instruction in many primary schools continues to bewilder children because it outruns their experience.
>
> (*ibid.*, p. 195)

Finally we should note repeated expressions of dissatisfaction with a subject-based curriculum. The modern primary school, the reader is told, 'insists that knowledge does not fall into neatly separate compartments' (p. 187); and the committee stresses that 'children's learning does not fit into subject categories' (p. 203).

The Plowden Report, unlike the Memorandum, goes on to deal with other matters like educational disadvantage and positive discrimination. But our concern here is with progressive pedagogy, and it is clear that these two documents issued powerful restatements of the central tenets of child-centred education. Schools, however, are not the kind of institutions that change overnight. So when Gerald Osborne declared in the year following its publication that the Primary Memorandum represented a 'revolution' (Osborne, 1966, p. 120), the most plausible interpretation of this claim is to locate the transformation not in school practice but in the official view of what ought to happen in primary classrooms. On the other hand, classroom practice is not conducted independently of this official view. Teaching is not a private transaction, but one that is open to inspection. While teachers are likely to be visited by inspectors on only a few occasions in the course of their careers, the knowledge that they *could* be inspected is bound to influence the way they work. Control by assessment, however, can only be effective if the agents to be controlled know what the assessor is looking for. Of the committee which produced the Primary Memorandum, seven were Her Majesty's Inspectors (HMIs). So what happened with the Memorandum's publication was that a new yardstick made its first public appearance.

Inspectors, of course, do not confine their attention to individual teachers: they judge schools, and therefore headteachers. Headteachers consequently can be counted on to encourage teachers in their schools to adopt practices which are officially favoured. Thus for the whole of primary education, the endorsement by these reports of the child-centred philosophy effectively created a new and powerful definition of good teaching.

Beyond the establishing of new standards, however, the subsequent impact of these reports must obviously be assessed in terms of classroom practice. Here it is important not to expect too much. Some have argued that Plowden's progressive pedagogy could not be fully implemented in primary classrooms (Galton, Simon and Croll, 1980). Against this we must set the fact that both Scottish and English committees saw themselves as building on existing practice in schools which they admired. The Secretary of State's preface to the Primary Memorandum describes it as providing 'an up-to-date appraisal of the best practices in primary schools in Scotland' (SED, 1965, p. iii). Seven headteachers sat on the Scottish committee. While the reasons for their appointment are not known, the assumption must be that the inspectorate saw the practices already in force in their schools as models which should inform the committee's deliberations. One of the headteachers has recorded that before his appointment to the committee his school had been visited by inspectors on several occasions (Farquharson, 1985).

The Plowden Report explains its strategy like this: 'In seeking answers . . . we draw attention to *the best practices we have found* as a pointer to the direction in which all schools should move' (CACE, 1967, p. 2, emphasis added). The committee's secretary, Maurice Kogan, explains that 'The Committee came to the conclusion that a strong minority of primary schools were successful in inculcating attitudes and relationships towards pupils that the Hadow Reports of 1931 and 1933 had thought appropriate in education' (Kogan, 1987, p. 14). The Plowden Report itself observed that 'Despite overcrowding and large classes, many post-war primary schools did much to enlarge children's experience and involve them more actively in the learning process – the main themes of the 1931 Report' (CACE, 1967, p. 190). Kogan reminds us that 'There were already excellent examples of 'open' primary schools already well known and well loved and, indeed, in such areas as the West Riding, Oxfordshire, Hertfordshire and Leicestershire, fully backed by leading administrators' (Kogan, 1987, p. 18).

The Director of Education for Leicestershire had been a member of the New Education Fellowship in the 1930s (Jones, 1987). Such primary schools had also attracted the interest of educationists from abroad. An American, Joseph Featherstone, published a series of articles under the title 'The primary school revolution in Britain' in *The New Republic* in 1967. After 1967 there was, according to a European observer, an endless series of cross-channel primary school pilgrimages to ILEA, Oxfordshire, Yorkshire and other places where one could observe 'Plowden in action' (Gruber, 1987, p. 58). A German edition of the Plowden Report was published in 1972. So although the discussion here is confined to developments in Britain, this does not make it a matter of parochial concern: for the ideas and their implementation became the centre of international attention.

However, it will be clear from what has been said that Plowden-style teaching predates Plowden, though we have no adequate information about the *extent* to which progressive pedagogy was already being practised. This makes it impossible to gauge the subsequent effect of the Plowden Report on the classroom. A popular line with academics has been to challenge the view that primary school practice altered fundamentally. In the 1987 issue of the *Oxford Review of Education*, which reviewed twenty years of Plowdenism, one critic (Scruton, 1987) claims that Plowden had a catastrophic effect on primary education while another (Gammage) claims that the primary revolution never actually happened. Much depends not just on definitions but on expectations. How much change could one reasonably expect to find? At what point does change become revolution? Attempts to ascertain the nature of classroom practice have produced mixed findings, but show clearly enough that child-centred thinking was making a significant impact.

One study identified twelve teaching styles. Type 1 was defined as follows:

> These teachers favour integration of subject matter, and, unlike most other groups, allow pupil choice of work, whether undertaken individually or in groups. Most allow pupils choice of seating. Less than half curb movement and talk. Assessment in all its forms – tests, grading, and homework – appears to be discouraged. Intrinsic motivation is favoured.
>
> (Bennett, 1976a, p. 45)

This was seen as the Plowden model and much was made of the fact that only 9 per cent of primary teachers were of this type. But importance might just as well have been attached to the influence of Plowden's thinking on other teachers who were unwilling to accept the whole package. Teachers in Type 2 and Type 3, for example, preferred integration of subject matter. In Type 4 'a high proportion allow pupil choice of work both in group and individual work'. The study found that 37 per cent of primary teachers agreed with the statement that 'Most pupils in upper junior school have sufficient maturity to choose a topic to study and carry it through' (*ibid.*, p. 59).

The ORACLE study in the Midlands produced similarly mixed findings. While there was little evidence of discovery learning being encouraged, pupils' work tended to be individualized, and classrooms were 'informally' organized (Simon and Willcocks, 1981). In a paper called 'The primary school revolution: myth or reality?', one of the principal researchers concludes: 'It seems that there has been a rather fundamental change in primary schools (perhaps more in infant than in junior schools) in terms of their internal structure, organization, and perhaps particularly in relationships' (Simon, 1980). It may be that Simon's reluctance to describe this change as 'revolutionary' is influenced by his suspicion that such language is sometimes used deliberately by conservatives to suggest something extreme or subversive which ought to be quashed.

In Scotland an investigation for the Scottish Council for Research in Education declared that in its initial investigations 'any teaching that could be described as "progressive" in any extreme sense was difficult if not impossible to find' (Powell, 1985, p. 6), although the researcher argued that much hangs here on the meaning of 'progressive'; and the concept is further obscured by the qualifying phrase 'in any extreme sense'. And his opening declaration has to be balanced against some of the observations made in the classrooms that were subsequently studied. From a series of reports we learn of classes which were 'active and happy' (*ibid.*, p. 84), 'open and informal' (p. 98) and where ' pupils were free to move, to work at a communal table, or to take back personal assignments to their own seats' (p. 77).

Comments on various teachers include:

- secured from individual pupils independent and responsible activity, activity often involving co-operation with other pupils (p. 76);
- able to require pupils to find out things for themselves (p. 77);
- strongly encouraged individual thinking and initiative (p. 79);
- was friendly and laughed a lot as she spoke (p. 82);
- maintained almost no social distance, allowing the pupils – particularly the more able ones – to relate to him on a basis of virtual equality (p. 101);
- was notable for . . . her responsiveness to pupils' interests, for her efforts to allow each child to work at his own level, for her working with individuals for substantial periods of time, for her skilled matching of responsibilities to pupil needs, and for the very marked informality of her relationships with her pupils (p. 109).

Finally, for the National Foundation for Educational Research, Michael Bassey asked 454 junior school teachers in Nottinghamshire to indicate the methods used in their classrooms for at least a quarter of the week. Twenty-four per cent listed 'classwork' as coming into this category: 6 per cent listed 'self-organized individual work'. Between these two extremes, however, there were different kinds of group work, and combinations of classwork with group work and group work with individualized work (Bassey, 1978). This particular study, unfortunately, may be unreliable because of its reliance on teachers' reports rather than observers' findings: it is generally recognized that teachers, while not guilty of deliberate falsification, tend to see what goes on in their classrooms in the light of their own aims. In practice this means that a teacher's and an observer's account of the same classroom proceedings will differ.

This points us to a different dimension where the Primary Memorandum and the Plowden Report seem likely to have made real impact: teachers' aims. A Schools Council investigation in 1972 asked primary teachers in England what they hoped to achieve with children by the time they left primary school. From a list of seventy-two suggested aims, the following three emerged as the most highly rated:

- children should be happy, cheerful and well balanced;
- they should enjoy school work and find satisfaction in their achievements;
- individuals should be encouraged to develop in their own ways.

(Ashton, Kneen and Holley, 1975, p. 58)

Attention has been drawn by R. F. Dearden and others to the way in which mastery of curricular content is apparently downgraded in this prioritization exercise. It is interesting to speculate on whether primary teachers would have responded in the same way twenty years earlier – or fifty years earlier.

A Scottish study found that primary teachers who qualified after 1965 were more favourably disposed to the child-centred approach than those trained earlier (Farquharson, 1984, p. 125). Findings like these, of course, are open to more than one explanation. One might point to the persuasiveness of the Primary Memorandum, which was required reading for all trainee teachers from the day it was published. More cynically, it might be suggested that teachers learn to adopt whatever approach seems to be endorsed by higher authority. Or it could be argued that such enthusiasm for new ways in education is simply a function of youth and inexperience, suggesting that with maturity teachers will return to more conservative ideas. The Plowden Report's own investigations also revealed that younger teachers tended to have more progressive opinions, to be less restrictive and more tolerant of noise.

In the final analysis, how far particular Plowden-approved practices have been implemented may be less important than the extent to which the Plowden way of *conceptualizing* primary education has been influential. Twenty years after the Report was published, this was one judgement: 'If Plowden has not been fully implemented, and its message has had to be clarified and modified with time, its inspiration continues to shape the goals of young teachers and their more experienced colleagues as well' (Halsey and Sylva, 1987, p. 11). The extent to which this is true in Scotland effectively gave primary education a unifying philosophy. In 1980 the Inspectorate declared that 'the way ahead is forward from the Memorandum' (SED, 1980, p. 54). Another document observed that 'most assessments of primary schools are done in terms of whether they have implemented the Memorandum' (COPE, 1983, p. 7). A 1986 report pointed out that in leaving primary school and beginning secondary, the pupil was moving from one philosophy-in-action to another: secondary education was still thought of as an aggregation of subjects, while primary education had been learner centred ever since the Primary Memorandum (PDC, 1986, p. 6). A later document speaks of the 'child-centred consensus' in Scottish primary education (COPE, 1987). In fact, wherever primary teachers came together to discuss, to learn, or even to disagree, the child-centred philosophy came to constitute a degree of common ground that could be taken for granted.

In all this there is a striking resemblance to some of the features of a religion. First, there is veneration for a good book. This volume sets out new ideals and standards in a way that is authoritative and persuasive. The advice that is given may be hard to follow – some may argue that it is impossible in the real world – yet adherents feel compelled to aspire towards following these prescriptions. The standards embodied in the book are used to judge institutions, public practices, other people and oneself. In the case of self-evaluation, this can never be entirely reassuring where the required practices are not easily carried out in full.

The 'good book' has an important inspirational function. To those who would have been attempting to conduct their teaching along such lines in any case, a worked-out theoretical rationale gives confidence. To those who have become persuaded by it, it gives the zeal that comes from having seen the true light. In some of the literature this effect is heightened by the habit of contrasting progressivism with bad, old ways which people must now reject and repent. And progressivism has some built-in emotional attractions: it is psychologically informed and therefore seems up to date, rational and enlightened; and it commits the teacher to some kind of respect for the child and the child's ways and thus makes the child-centred teacher morally admirable.

So it is not surprising that in primary education, adherence – whether zealous or lukewarm – became very widespread. Progressivism was the new orthodoxy. As with religion, this has the great advantage of unifying the people. All of us in primary education knew where we were going and what we ought to be doing: we were all on the side of the child. We knew that these ideas were shared by our fellow educators. An introduction to these beliefs and values became part of a trainee teacher's socialization.

It remains to consider why it was that progressivism became the accepted view. This chapter will conclude by reviewing some of the factors that may have enabled child-centred education to achieve this position of the established religion of the primary teacher from the mid-1960s onwards.

One important enabling condition was that at this time Britain enjoyed widespread prosperity. Unemployment was low and parents had every reason to assume that when their children left school they would be able to get jobs without much difficulty. Where there is anxiety about employment there tends to be pressure on schools to pursue narrow vocational ends. Where the reverse holds, parents are prepared to entertain broader goals for their children's development and they become less apprehensive about innovative approaches.

What gave positive encouragement to the introduction of progressive education in this period was a new climate of ideas whose character was generally described by its supporters as 'permissive' (though this term later acquired a pejorative tone). First, there was an increased emphasis on the individual's right to self-determination – to choose, to think, to decide for oneself – an idea which has since acquired the status of unremarkable common sense, but which in the 1960s had the power to appear radical, threatening and newsworthy. Mick Jagger of the Rolling Stones was typical: 'It's when authority won't allow something that I dig in. I'm against anything that interferes with individual freedom. As a non-conformist I won't accept what other people say is right. And there are hundreds like me, thousands' (quoted in Hoggart *et al.*, 1969, p. 15).

This new-found confidence in one's right to self-determination produced a heady truculence towards authority figures and an enthusiasm for exposing their pretensions. For the first time, the Queen was openly criticized: though what was significant was that public uproar could be created by what were generally only mildly disparaging remarks. Speaking the unthinkable and flouting the conventional became for some a popular sport. For others, like Malcolm Muggeridge, it became almost a profession. In 1960 scandalizing people was easy work. With politicians and the police being derided and ridiculed, and God being declared dead, the exercise of authority became a fraught and uncomfortable business since respectfulness could no longer be taken for granted. In this new social climate a move away from authoritarian styles of teaching became inevitable.

More pertinent, perhaps, to our treatment of children was the increased acceptance of Freudian strictures on repressiveness. While the general public knew as little as ever about Freud, there was a general acceptance of the idea that harsh discipline or undue restraint imposed on the young was not conducive to healthy emotional development but was likely to have undesirable repercussions. Adults themselves felt a new entitlement to the good things in life, including sexual gratification – a goal which required the overthrowing of old inhibiting taboos and which was facilitated by the availability of the contraceptive pill. School was seen as having been instrumental in fostering a mindless acceptance of traditional morality. For their children, people now expected something better and more positive. The hypocrisies of the old order were to be swept away by a younger, better generation of which John F. Kennedy became an ill-chosen symbol. Peace was to be given a chance: all that was needed was love. Even drug-taking was viewed optimistically as a way of putting you in touch with other areas of yourself, a way of liberating yourself from restricted modes of thought.

Ernest Gellner has drawn attention to the way in which the ideas of psychoanalysis have become 'the dominant idiom for the discussion of the human personality and of human relationships ' (Gellner, 1985, p. 5). One of these ideas is that the infant psyche is extremely fragile, liable to permanent damage if handled in a way that is insensitive to its needs and nature. This demand for teacher sensitivity is much in evidence in the Primary Memorandum. So too is the advocacy of psychologically informed, non-punitive reactions to undesirable behaviour:

> In an atmopshere of security and affection . . . and in the hands of teachers who understand the developing pattern of his [the pupil's] emotions, his increasing desire for independence, which occasionally reveals itself in hostility and rebelliousness against authority, can be diverted into rewarding channels, and used to motivate him in the pursuit of his own education.
>
> (SED, 1965, p. 6)

This interest in the psychological make-up of the young child was further encouraged by a strong, if sometimes naive and superficial, egalitarian movement which influenced thinking about policy in many fields at this time. The guiding sentiment here was not too distant from Rousseau's Utopian egalitarianism and Dewey's anti-élitism. If the educational system was to make a significant contribution to the emergence of a fairer and more equal society, it was thought that the necessary changes would have to start with *young* children: attempts to promote greater equality at secondary school level seemed unlikely to be able to tackle the roots of the problem of gross inequalities in achievement. Primary education therefore had the unusual experience of finding itself the centre of attention. It became clear to the liberal and humane that while much positive thinking was being implemented at the infant stages, the later years of the primary school were dominated and restricted by an examination system that was required to assess the fitness of children for different types of secondary education. Variously called the 'eleven plus', the 'qualifying' or the 'control' examination, this (like any other externally administered assessment) tended to focus the curriculum on its own requirements. Since the task of this exam was generally seen as one of selecting pupils who were capable of pursuing a formal academic educa-tion at secondary level, the advanced stages of the primary curriculum themselves tended to be formal and academic. Throughout this period, however, there were increasing demands for a comprehensive system of secondary schooling. When the selection process finally collapsed under the weight of egalitarian sentiment, the major obstacle to the liberalization of the primary curriculum was removed. What we may call the Plowdenization of primary education is thus closely linked to the development of comprehensive secondary schools.

Giving an account of the Plowdenization process, however, is not the main purpose of this book. The changed thinking in primary education has been outlined in order to set the scene for a more particular investigation.

We have noted that today's primary schooling can be traced to yesterday's books, with training colleges performing the intermediary role of fostering child-centred ideas in student teachers. From the range of theoretical literature surveyed earlier, two writers can be identified as intellectual giants by any standards – Rousseau and Dewey. What is significant for our purposes is that both were philosophers as well as advocates of child-centred education, a fusion of thought that showed no signs of internal tension.

In the 1960s and 70s, however, philosophers of education were at loggerheads with child-centred education. Furthermore, despite the anti-progressive tone of the new philosophy of education, it featured prominently in college curricula. How this came about will be explained in the chapters which follow.

6

PHILOSOPHY AND R. S. PETERS

We have seen that child-centred education is old in terms of theory, having been argued for by philosophers and others over the last two hundred years, but, equally clearly, it is new in terms of practice, having been first established in Britain on a mass scale in the 1960s and 1970s. At the same time as these changes were taking place in primary schools, philosophy of education was itself undergoing a transformation. Instead of contributing to the development of progressive educational theory, philosophers became critical of it. Who were the philosophers of this period and do they matter? Why did they think like this? And are the arguments convincing? Answers to these questions will be put forward in Chapters 6, 7 and 8. First, however, a bit of intellectual scene-setting is required, because developments in philosophy of education were closely related to prior developments in philosophy itself.

In the period leading up to the 1960s, philosophy of education was not a prominent feature of the intellectual landscape: it had fallen into disrepute, a casualty of the 'revolution' in philosophy. In the middle of this century there had been much discussion among philosophers about the nature of philosophy. The view which prevailed about what philosophers could and could not legitimately do excluded many traditional kinds of philosophical enterprise. One of these was philosophy of education, at least as it had been generally practised.

One might say that the post-war 'revolution' in British philosophy began in 1936 with a premature bombshell dropped by A. J. Ayer in the shape of *Language, Truth and Logic*. The shrapnel went everywhere. Ayer was twenty-five, the same age Hume was when he published his *Treatise of Human Nature*. Unlike the *Treatise*, however, *Language, Truth and Logic* was a short, compelling read; and it certainly did not fall, as Hume complained, 'stillborn from the press'. Its central claim was that for a statement to be meaningful it must be possible in principle to verify it, or at least establish its probability, by gathering evidence through sense experience. Statements which fall outside this category were declared to be senseless, and therefore could not be said to be either true or false. The only exceptions to this rule were those statements whose truth is guaranteed by the meaning of the terms used. In this the philosophical world was witnessing a restatement of an earlier categorization developed by Hume who put the point in a celebrated purple passage which Ayer quotes:

> If we take in our hand any volume; of divinity, or school metaphysics, for instance; let us ask, Does it contain any abstract reasoning concerning quantity or number? No. Does it contain any experimental reasoning concerning matter of fact and existence? No. Commit it then to the flames. For it can contain nothing but sophistry and illusion.
>
> (Ayer, 1936, p. 54)

Into the category of sophistry and illusion Ayer put not just our ideas of God and immortality, but moral and aesthetic notions as well. 'Good', 'wrong' and 'beautiful' were seen as pseudo-concepts whose function was merely to express the speaker's feeling or attitude towards something.

Ayer maintained that the style of his own argument in *Language, Truth and Logic* exemplified a particular conception of philosophy which he wished to advance. Philosophizing, he claimed, was not a searching for first principles, but was a matter of analysis. Ayer thought it possible in principle (and also desirable) for philosophers to reach agreement over the problems they tackled, for philosophical disputes arose only when one side or the other committed a logical error. The detection of this error would, he thought, resolve the dispute and produce philosophical harmony. Regardless of the theoretical merits of this claim, it is difficult to reconcile such a picture with the realities of philosophical arguing. Characteristically, if error is conceded by the proponent of a view, then, rather than endorsing the critic's view, a philosopher is likely to seek a new or revised defence of the original position. It is hard to see any reason for viewing this as an improper move which discredits philosophy as a discipline.

Despite his own distaste for the existence of philosophical 'parties', Ayer's book has itself the qualities of a devastating and passionate piece of polemic. The force of this polemic dealt heavy blows to philosophy of education and political philosophy. Traditionally, enquirers in these fields have sought to justify forms of human relationships, institutions and transactions, and have tried to demonstrate that some forms are more desirable than others. The message from *Language, Truth and Logic* is twofold: (i) this is not a proper kind of activity for philosophers; and (ii) any conclusions reached about the nature of a good society or a good education are strictly meaningless. For philosophers, all that was left in the realm of values was to examine further the nature of value judgements. Moral philosophy was reconceived as a study of the language and logic of moral discourse: tackling questions of moral substance was out of order.

Ayer saw himself operating within the British empiricist tradition and he mentions approvingly the work of various philosophers from Locke to the then existing publications of Wittgenstein. Within this school, however, Russell, both the Mills, and Locke himself all applied themselves to educational problems including the question of what ought to be taught. Such a question seems to offend Ayer's rules for philosophers on two counts: (i) it involves an attempt to resolve a question of substance, and perhaps to establish some basic principles; and (ii) since it involves a value concept, it (and any answer it elicits) is strictly meaningless. One possible response here might be to say that when Locke is arguing a case about education he is not writing in his capacity as a philosopher, or he is not doing philosophy. Russell certainly deals quite separately with logic and with education, and in quite different styles. On the other hand, if we were to take Plato as an example, we would find that educational questions, metaphysical questions and political questions are all being discussed in one work, the *Republic*; and his answers to these different sorts of questions are closely related to each other.

It might, of course, be argued that it is unfair to take an example from a period when it was possible for one person to cover the whole range of knowledge, and when knowledge had not become widely differentiated. However, this perception of a close relationship between philosophy and education is not peculiar to ancient times. John Dewey, who was writing from the end of the nineteenth century onwards, was quite explicit in connecting these areas of enquiry almost to the point of making them identical: 'If a [philosophical] theory makes no difference in educational endeavour, it must be artificial . . . philosophy may even be defined *as the general theory of education*' (Dewey, 1916, p. 328, author's emphasis).

This kind of claim is totally at odds with the conception of philosophy which Ayer outlines. Such has been the influence of the new model, however, that in the 1960s a commentary on Plato could be prefaced like this: 'because we think that some parts of the *Republic*, whatever other interest they may have, have no philosophical interest, we have said nothing about them; for example, there is no discussion of Plato's views on school education' (Cross and Woozley, 1964, p. v). There seems little doubt that this observation would have left Plato baffled.

As we have seen, Ayer's philosophical analysis laid waste whole areas of discourse. But not all analytical philosophy did this. In particular we must note the approach associated with Wittgenstein's later teaching which had widespread influence long before it appeared in book form as *Philosophical Investigations* (1953). Essentially this involved an attempt to understand language by studying the ways in which it was used, reflecting a new awareness of the variety of functions which language served. Gone was the view that the proper purpose of language was to describe or label physical phenomena, and that it was this relationship of language to observed things that gave language meaning. Such an account of meaningfulness was seen as too restrictive: language could be meaningful in all sorts of different ways. Instead of trying to rule out whatever failed to fit the scientific paradigm, it came to be seen that there were various intellectual traditions (of which science was one), each with its own rules of discourse. So to declare religious statements to be meaningless on the grounds that they could not be verified empirically was a case of applying inappropriate criteria.

This view clearly involved a new respect for the way people use language. Instead of ordinary language being seen as in need of wholesale revision, or (as Russell thought) replacement by a more accurate philosophical language, it was often the statements of philosophers that were seen as needing to be corrected in the light of ordinary usage. Debates about whether free will is possible, for example, were explicable in terms of philosophers' failure to appreciate that we already have well-established criteria for distinguishing between actions freely performed and actions performed under duress.

Such a plain-man view, of course, can be highly conservative. For philosophers to take this view seems to involve the risk of putting themselves out of business: what would be left for them to do? Influential philosophers like J. L. Austin occupied themselves with pointing out how particular expressions could be deceptive. In an attempt to sort these things out, he presided over a series of meetings – today we would no doubt call them 'workshops' – where small points of language use were examined by the group in meticulous detail. Austin was impressed by the idea that subjects like psychology had historically been developed within philosophy before establishing themselves as independent disciplines. In linguistic analysis he saw philosophy giving birth to an embryonic science of language. Significantly he thought a good strategy for philosophers would be for a group of them to agree to work on different aspects of the same problem and then assemble their various findings – essentially the model for much scientific research. Austin's admirers (and there were many in the world of academic philosophy) disdained the partisan polemic in favour of skilled and dispassionate dissection – the same spirit and style which Ayer's positivist tract had advocated if not exemplified.

Technique divides the world into those who have it and those who do not, and it is revealing that one account of the philosophical revolution uses the term 'layman' to indicate people who are not professional philosophers (Flew, 1951, p. 2). Inevitably there is a danger that in this way of thinking the difference between the skills of the professional and the non-professional becomes exaggerated: in the writings of the new philosophy there seems little in the style of the argument that could not be acquired by an interested 'layman'. Yet Antony Flew is not above persuading fellow professionals to join the ranks of the new philosophy by issuing some disconcerting warnings. Asserting that what makes verbal sense may nevertheless be logical nonsense, Flew argued:

> As such discoveries have been developed and applied in field after field, enterprises of metaphysical construction have seemed less and less practicable, less and less respectable. For anyone who has seen how much muddle and perplexity, how much paradox and absurdity has already been traced back to its tainted sources in misleading idiom, or in unexplained and unnoticed distortions of standard English, must suspect that any further metaphysical construction which he might be tempted to erect would soon meet with a similar humiliating and embarrassing debacle under the assaults of the new 'logic and critic'.
>
> (Flew, 1951, p. 9)

Here readers are clearly being told that unless they do their philosophizing in the new style, they will appear academically disreputable and end up making fools of themselves. There appears to have been a remarkably high rate of conversion among the ranks of professional independent thinkers to the changed conception of philosophy. Perhaps due to an uncertainty about their academic place in a scientific world, philosophers seem to have been very responsive to demands that they conform to the new rules and pathologically fearful of being accused of saying something meaningless or absurd.

In this atmosphere, large areas of philosophy simply ceased. Very little political philosophy, for example, was being written. In 1956 Peter Laslett wrote in a widely read volume, 'Political philosophy is dead', though he did seem to entertain the hope of a second coming (Laslett, 1956). Five years later, Isaiah Berlin was still ruminating on whether to certify the demise of this discipline, but felt able to forecast 'new and unpredictable developments' (Berlin, 1961). In fact it was in the field of political philosophy that the first cautious attempts were made to reconnect philosophy to social institutions. One of the early works here, *Social Principles and the Democratic State*, was co-authored by R. S. Peters while he was still working in a university philosophy department. From 1962 Peters occupied the chair of philosophy of education at the London University Institute of Education where his colleagues included Paul Hirst and Robert Dearden. All three held similar views and proceeded by means of similar (and sometimes identical) arguments. They produced a significant amount of new writing from the 1960s onwards, and remain today the best known philosophers of education in Britain.

In the light of the 'revolution' in philosophy, how did the new philosophers of education view their subject? In a widely read outline of the discipline Peters observed: 'The distinctive feature of philosophical inquiries which accounts for the spectatorial role of the philosopher, is their second-order character' (Peters, 1966b, p. 60). He was convinced that analytic philosophy 'had much to offer to education' (Peters, 1983, p. 36). But what exactly could be achieved through second-order studies conducted by someone confined to a spectator's role?

> a much clearer grasp of the fundamental issues underlying current controversies is made possible by mapping the area of the concepts and revealing the contours of the criteria built into them. But a detached and clear-sighted view of the shape of issues and institutions is all that conceptual analysis provides. It cannot of itself determine the lines of practical policy.
>
> (Peters, 1966a, p. 45)

What had previously passed muster as philosophy of education was viewed as outmoded: it was simply no longer intellectually respectable. Peters and others like him repeatedly expressed disapproval of what was said to be the kind of philosophy of education that featured on teacher-training courses. A recurring theme was that the subject was taught by people who were not familiar with the changed face of philosophy – a criticism which was sometimes delivered in a tone which verged on academic sneering. Thus Peters: 'Many philosophers who have been brought up in the "revolution" . . . are . . . rather aghast when they encounter what is often called "philosophy of education" with its rather woolly chatter about "growth" "wholeness" "maturity" "discipline" "experience" "creativeness" "needs" "interests" and "freedom"' (Peters, 1964, pp. 141–2). Hirst criticized 'The production of educational sermons intended to commend certain specific aims and to exhort students and teachers to the ardent pursuit of them' (Hirst, 1966, p. 29). Peters also claimed that

> Few professional philosophers would now think it is their function to provide such high-level directives for education or for life; indeed one of their main preoccupations has been to lay bare such aristocratic pronouncements under the analytic guillotine. They cast themselves in the more mundane Lockean role of underlabourers in the garden.
>
> (Peters, 1966a, p. 15)

Outdoing these, another writer (at least by implication) likens some existing versions of philosophy of education to a load of horse manure!

> I spoke earlier of the need to clean the stables. This is particularly pressing in educational theory for the eclecticism and broad synthetic treatments have spawned vagueness, ambiguity and pseudo-problems . . . [due to] the failure, on the part of workers in the philosophy of education to recognize or to use the gains made in recent philosophy.
>
> (Archambault, 1965, p. 8)

Clearly it was felt to be important for the new philosophy of education to distance itself from what had gone before. But, rhetoric aside, exactly what was being rejected? Four years after getting his chair, Peters spelled out his detailed objections to unacceptable versions of philosophy of education as professed in British teacher training (Peters, 1966b, p. 62 ff.).

The first approach to be criticized is labelled 'principles of education'. This is said to involve the enunciation of values and principles of teaching. It is, complains Peters, philosophical only in the everyday sense employed in questions like 'What is his philosophy of education?' – the kind of talk, we are told, which makes the professional philosopher wince. The formulation of educational principles cannot be a philosopher's job, according to Peters, partly because these draw on value judgements, on areas where 'the philosopher is not an authority *qua* philosopher'.

Nevertheless, there is clearly something odd in the idea of anyone writing about education in a way that avoids all value judgements. Firstly, the writer must think education is worth writing about – does it not, after all, concern the development of our children, our society's next generation? Anyone who responds positively to this point will be anxious not just that children develop, but that they should develop in the best possible way – though how this is defined may be a matter for debate. The values of many educational philosophers – as well as sociologists and historians – clearly inform their work, and this does not suggest that their work is defective. Indeed there is much to be said for a writer's values being indicated openly so that they can be readily recognized. Where they lurk beneath the surface, they may remain concealed from the unwary reader, and sometimes from the writer as well. In Chapter 7, Peters' own values will be highlighted and discussed.

The second form of philosophy of education which Peters criticizes is described as the 'history of educational ideas'. Peters may be right in complaining that such college courses were too fragmented, and that they tended to neglect the differences between the conditions of today and the conditions which prevailed when historical figures were writing about education. If these criticisms are valid, they show that courses of this kind need to be improved, not that they should be abandoned. But Peters' more substantial objection is that books like the *Republic* 'are, strictly speaking, works in general theory of education' (Peters, 1966b, p. 65). This is argued on the grounds that they include value judgements and empirical observations as well as philosophical argument. Elsewhere Peters makes further disparaging remarks on the historical approach to philosophy, asserting that modern philosophers are

> aghast when they learn that students very often are brought up on an antiquated diet of Plato, Rousseau and Froebel – perhaps with a dash of Dewey to provide a final obfuscation of issues. It is as if a course on educational psychology consisted mainly of snippets from Aristotle, Locke, James Mill, Herbart and Thorndike.
>
> (Peters, 1964, p. 142)

This analogy with psychology is, as I shall try to show, a misleading one, but the passage serves to show how determined Peters was at this time to distance himself from historical work. However, 'pure' philosophers seldom lose sight of Plato and Kant, and many philosophy degree courses are taught primarily through the work of such major figures of the past. This suggests that history of philosophy is not something separate from philosophy itself in the way that, say, the history of mathematics may be separate from mathematics. Ignorance of the subject's history would be a major handicap to becoming a first-class philosopher, though this would probably not hold good for becoming a first-class mathematician. If the history of mathematics were taught to mathematicians, the purpose would be to let them see how their subject developed. Courses in the history of philosophy, however, have a further purpose: to consider whether or not (or how far) what was said by Kant or John Stuart Mill was right. The claims of many historical figures can still be taken seriously and grappled with: their theses remain, one might say, 'live options'. As one moves into science, however, it is easy to see that historical theories have become demonstrably false or inadequate. In so far as psychology is a science, therefore, it would certainly be inappropriate for a psychology course to consist of a study of psychological writing of the eighteenth or nineteenth centuries. It does not follow from this that philosophy courses should not feature work done in these periods.

So far, this account of the new philosophy of education has been developed in negative terms: one can learn much about its character by examining what it rejects. What, however, was there in earlier writers for Peters to admire? He explains:

> The pioneer in approaching educational issues from the standpoint of 'the revolution in philosophy' was undoubtedly C. D. Hardie in his *Truth and Fallacy in Educational Theory* which was first pub-lished in 1942 . . . . In this he employed tools of analysis fashioned mainly by G. E. Moore and C. D. Broad
>
> (Peters, 1966b, p. 69)

Here, then, was the approved modern analytic approach. Hardie's book, however, was a slim volume which did not take the subject very far. Noting in particular that Hardie offered no analysis of the concept of education itself, Peters resolved to remedy the omission, and the analysis of this concept became the main focus of his early writing. This analysis forms the substance of the first chapter of *Ethics and Education* (1966); and a later book, *The Logic of Education*, co-authored by Hirst (Hirst and Peters, 1970), is described in the authors' introduction as 'a positive thesis about the implications of an analysis of "education"'. Although this is seen as conceptual analysis in the approved philosophical style, it is regarded not as a self-contained academic exercise but as a piece of reasoning that has practical importance and value. Peters speaks of the 'urgent necessity' of getting 'clearer about the concept of "education"', and he worries about teachers who are suffering from 'conceptual blight' (Peters, 1963, p. 82). This last expression suggests, in modern philosophical style, that those who take a different view of the meaning of education are committing a logical error.

What, then, does a true understanding of the concept reveal? In formal terms, education is said to involve the intentional transmission of something worth while, or (an alternative rendering) the transmission of 'things of ultimate value'. The kind of argument employed here is the observation that 'It would be a logical contradiction to say that . . . in educating his son a man was attempting nothing worthwhile.' If we want to argue with this, we might claim that it was perfectly intelligible to say that the emptiness and purposelessness of some people's lives was due to their education (perhaps on the grounds that their education had made them into complete sceptics). Peters here might be driven to make a distinction between 'real' education and what was incorrectly seen as education – a kind of linguistic legislation which reveals the prescriptive element in this type of conceptual analysis.

Further, Peters wants to say that the content of education consists of things worth doing, or learning, or experiencing for their own sakes, not as a means to achieving something else. Hence the function of education should not be understood in terms of aims and goals external to the educational process itself. Peters seems to have two reasons for taking this line. The first is a desire to distinguish education from training, since training is seen as having only limited objectives. The second is a logical point. If education involves the transmission of things of ultimate value, it is odd to ask 'But what is this transmission *for*?' There is a connection between these points: for the test of a good training is that it equips one to do something else – perhaps a particular kind of job. But not everything can function as a means to an end. Somewhere something has got to carry with it its own justification. Peters believes that education comes into this category. Hence Peters' paper, 'Must an educator have an aim?' Here he complains about suggested aims like 'self-development' (which he describes as a 'metaphysical whistle in the dark') firstly on the grounds that they are vague and ambiguous.

> For what sort of self is to be realized? What quality of life is worth perpetuating? Teachers surely care whether or not poetry rather than push-pin is perpetuated, to use a time-honoured example. The problem of justifying such 'higher' activities is one of the most difficult and persistent problems in ethics. But talk about self-realization and other such omnibus 'ends' does more than obscure it; it also encourages an *instrumental* way of looking at the problem of justification. For a nebulous end is invented which such activities are supposed to lead up to, because it is erroneously assumed that education must be justified by reference to an end which is extrinsic to it. The truth is much more that there is a quality of life embedded in the activities which constitute educa-

tion, and that 'self-realization' can be explicated only by reference to such activities.

(Peters, 1959, p. 131, author's emphasis)

Having deprived himself of metaphysical whistles (perhaps these might include such popular perennials as citizenship, common sense, and good character), is there some other way in which Peters can delineate the nature of education? His method is to invoke the notion of 'the educated man'.

Before considering the way in which the educated person is defined, we should consider whether this is a sound and legitimate explanatory device. It might be instructive here to draw an analogy with the Christian notion of 'conversion'. Both 'conversion' and 'education' (as Peters is using it here) are what have come to be called 'achievement' words. But in both cases, there seems to be scope for asking what is the point of striving for such achievements. If we put ourselves within the framework of religious thinking we can see that from the missionary's point of view such a question must seem odd. What kind of an answer could be given? The trouble with conversion, as with Peters' notion of education, is that it appears to people in the business to stand in no need of justification. It might be said that the point of converting people was to glorify God – but if the point of everything is to glorify God, then this tells us little. It might be said that the aim of conversion was to get more people to accept the faith, but this would be a trivial restatement of the meaning of the word 'conversion'. One way in which it would seem possible to say something illuminating would be by describing the people who have undergone conversion: they see where they once were blind, they enjoy a promise of eternal life, they know peace, and so on. These are presented as desirable states of mind possessed by converts: each attribute is part of what is involved in having faith. If the sceptic still sees no point in conversion, there is nothing more that can be said. Similarly, once it is accepted that education has no aim beyond itself, the only way to achieve an understanding of its purpose is to look at what is involved in having been educated.

For Peters, an educated person must be knowledgeable; but it is not sufficient to have assimilated large quantities of information. There must also be some understanding of how facts are established, of what counts as relevant evidence or sound argument, and of how rational enquiry is conducted. Further, the knowledge acquired must have a vital attraction for the knower and must affect the way the world is subsequently viewed. Peters illustrates his thesis like this:

> It is possible for a man to know a lot of history in the sense that he can give correct answers to questions in class-rooms and examinations; yet this might never affect the way in which he looks at buildings and institutions around him. We might describe such a man as 'knowledgeable' but we would not describe him as 'educated'.

(Peters, 1966a, p. 31)

Finally, to count as educated, one requires 'cognitive perspective': this means having some worked-out understanding of how the different areas of knowledge fit together in the general scheme of things. Peters' various qualifications, however, should not distract attention from the central place given in his account of education to the acquisition of knowledge.

Some comment is necessary on the nature of the argument so far. It is very easy for the reader to focus on the correctness or otherwise of Peters' criteria for distinguishing between people who are educated and people who are not, without considering whether such a distinction is sensible or useful. The reason for the appeal of the educated/uneducated distinction may lie in the popular identification of education with the transactions of specialized institutions like schools and colleges. In the public mind there is probably one group above all who can be seen as educated – university graduates, people who have been right through the system and who have 'done well' even in the most demanding and prestigious institutions.

What is often meant in calling people educated is that they have learned the kind of stuff that has traditionally been taught in educational institutions. Peters' analysis thus invokes the powerful backing of common usage. His argument frequently takes the form 'We would only call people educated if they . . .' or 'We would not call people educated unless they . . .'. But if, as I have suggested, our criteria for applying the epithet 'educated' are heavily influenced by the public's experience of undergoing schooling and its curriculum, then this kind of argument has a built-in conservative bias. In broader terms, as Robin Barrow has argued, 'To understand how words are commonly or generally used is to understand how people commonly or generally think. It does not touch upon the quality of that thought, which may be incoherent, confused, incorrect or plain silly' (Barrow, 1982, p. 51).

We might further ask of the educated person (as defined by Peters) whether, with his or her breadth of disinterested learning, this is not some altogether exceptional person. If this is what schools aim to produce, then their success rate must be rather low. Conversely, if schooling is not a massive failure, should we have a more modest, less ambitious model of what it is to be educated? Here it is tempting to subscribe to Raymond Williams' exasperated view:

> The level indicated by 'educated' has been continually adjusted to leave the majority of people who have received an education below it. It remains remarkable that after nearly a century of universal education in Britain the majority of the population should be seen as 'uneducated' or 'half-educated', but whether 'educated people' think of this with self-congratulation or self-reproach, or with impatience at the silliness of the usage, is for them to say.
>
> (Williams, 1976, pp. 95–6)

Instead of arguing about the *level* at which to make these distinctions, we might equally complain that Peters' criteria are drawn from only one *dimension*. It has been argued that Peters' exposition leaves us in a position where we can say of people that they are well educated (meaning that they have a highly developed understanding) but they cannot organize their own lives, cannot relate to other people, are neurotic and miserable, are incompetent in all practical and technical matters and have, through neglect, turned themselves into physical wrecks (Downie, Loudfoot and Telfer, 1974). In keeping with this kind of criticism, child-centred theorists have advanced the importance of other considerations such as the ability to do creative work and the capacity for self-direction and self-determination. In *The Logic of Education*, however, Peters and Hirst argue that 'underlying all the more sophisticated objectives such as autonomy, creativeness and critical thought, there must necessarily be the achievements of objective experience, knowledge and understanding' (Hirst and Peters, 1970, pp. 61–2). In fact, the nearest this argument comes to a consideration of creativeness is this: 'only in so far as one has the relevant knowledge and forms of reasoning can a person be creative or critical in, say, atomic physics' (*ibid*., p. 62). It is a common academic failing, manifest in psychology textbooks, to insist on construing 'creativity' as a capacity for problem-solving. While the point as quoted is indisputable, it is less clear how far such a requirement would hold good for creative work in philosophy or poetry let alone in the visual arts.

Suppose, however, it is conceded that the attainment of alternative goals like creativity does require the prior acquisition of knowledge: whether this means that the argument works depends on what Peters wants it to do. It may establish the necessity of a cognitive element in the curriculum, but it will not establish the intrinsic value of knowledge: for the acquisition of this degree of understanding may be held to be important only in so far as it permits the fulfilment of these other goals. Peters does, however, produce another argument for the value of knowledge, and to this we now turn.

What Peters calls his 'transcendental' argument appears as a justification of school subjects. He declares: 'Arguments must be given for initiating children into activities and forms of awareness such as science and poetry rather than bingo and horror films' (Peters, 1966a, p. 92). Diplomatically, however, while Peters aims to establish a distinction of value between the activities which he thinks make up education and activities which are non-educational, he does not expect to hit on an argument which will differentiate between those subjects which are seen to have a legitimate place in the curriculum: 'It might be possible . . . to show why history and literary appreciation are more worthwhile than bingo, and bridge; but it does not follow that there must also be reasons for saying that history is more worthwhile than literary appreciation' (Peters, 1966a, p. 144). As things turn out, however, Peters' expectations do not seem to be fulfilled, as will become evident shortly.

It will be clear from what has already been said that Peters is not looking for arguments which will justify curriculum activities as means to ulterior ends. So one possible line would be to point to the pleasure or satisfaction such activities provide for the participants. Peters is reluctant to rely on this kind of approach for several reasons. First, like so many modern philosophers, Peters sees an unbridgeable logical gulf between what is desired and what is desirable. Secondly, since much pleasure is derived from bingo and horror films, an argument from satisfaction might elevate activities in which Peters sees little value. Peters declines to endorse Mill's principle which declares that the superior of two activities can be conclusively identified by allowing an individual experience of both and then asking which he prefers: again Peters rejects this test on the rather odd grounds that it might produce the wrong answer. And, at the end of the day, this kind of approach provides no defence against the sceptic who says 'So what?'

In fact it is the imaginary sceptic who points the way to a solution for Peters. Suppose the sceptic says 'Is there really any value in activities like science and history?' or 'Why should I esteem scientific enquiry more highly than a game of bingo?' The answer is that scientific enquiry is committed to ascertaining what is true – and so, as revealed by the questioning, is the sceptic. Since sceptics think it important to probe the justification of people's claims, they must hold in esteem those disciplines like science which do this so successfully (Peters, 1966a, pp. 164–5).

This argument, however, seems far from satisfactory. It has been pointed out that it only works if people *do* ask the sceptical question, and ask it in a serious spirit – otherwise the questioner may have no commitment to the value of intellectual enquiry (Downie *et al.*, 1974, p. 45 ff.). Even if the argument did demonstrate the incoherence of a rational rejection of rational enquiry, it could not exclude the possibility of different kinds of activity (games perhaps) being justified in different ways which might establish their superior value. Further, the argument fails to produce any justification for anything in the curriculum except those activities whose function is to ascertain the truth. Many school subjects appear to fall outside this category, including some traditionally central ones like languages and literature. So even if the argument worked for science, it would do nothing to establish the value of music.

Finally, it is necessary to comment on the 'feel' of the transcendental argument. It is essentially an ingenious logical device which may reassure defenders of the traditional school curriculum, and which can be used to fend off any sceptical challenge to their established views. It is quite lacking in the compelling power one might expect of an argument which purports to demonstrate how young people should occupy 15,000 hours of their lives. In this it resembles proofs of God's existence which are invariably invented by those who have never doubted the conclusion and which are totally unconvincing for anyone who has ever entertained such doubts.

This discussion will be concluded by pointing to two different kinds of challenge which might be mounted. The first is the position favoured by some radical child-centred thinkers, which maintains that it matters little what children learn so long as they are learning. When Peters speaks of 'the activities which constitute education' he is trying to divide experience in a way that makes scant sense. All activities have some educative potential; and children learn a great deal outside any school curriculum. Ivan Illich has compared the distinction between educational activities and non-educational activities to the clerical insistence on dividing the world into what is sacred and what is profane instead of seeing the religious as an aspect of the secular. And he complains that as a result both domains become distorted: education becomes unworldly and the world becomes non-educational (Illich, 1973, p. 44). This kind of argument has never been taken seriously by philosophers of education who prefer to dismiss Illich's writing as 'romantic ramblings' (Dearden, Hirst and Peters, 1975, p. x).

A second kind of challenge might accept the legitimacy of Peters' endeavour to establish which activities are most worth while but reject his conclusion. First one could note the rather loaded examples which he uses to illustrate possible alternatives: science and poetry versus bingo and horror films. He might have chosen rather more impressive examples from the fields of games and the theatrical arts. Secondly, we should observe that activities in both these fields meet Peters' requirement that they have intrinsic value and can properly be pursued for their own sakes. Peters is conscious of this second point, and this leads him to explain why, despite the intrinsic value of both, games are inferior to curriculum activities.

Curriculum activities can be shown to be superior because (i) they 'contribute much to the quality of living', (ii) they 'have a wide-ranging cognitive content', and (iii) they 'illuminate other areas of life' (Peters, 1966a. p. 159). While (i) is not in serious dispute, this claim leaves open the possibility that a greater contribution might be made by other activities. Claim (ii) presupposes an acceptance of the view that cognitive content is the criterion on which the value of an activity is to be judged: this, however, is the issue supposedly under consideration. It is subsequently argued that if games promoted the acquisition of knowledge then it would be proper to view them as educational. Claim (iii) invokes a good reason for seeing some activities as valuable. But is it really plausible to claim that the *illumination* of other areas of life is the most worthwhile activity of all? What of the other activities that go to make up our lives and which curriculum activities are said to illuminate? Is the work of the sculptor of less value than the work of the art critic? It will now be shown that this is the position to which Peters is committed.

The activities of what we would today call sports sociologists and sports psychologists – academics who are described by Peters as really interested not in cricket as such but 'in the behaviour of men as exemplified in cricket' – are seen by Peters as more worth while than the activities of the cricketers themselves, who should be seen as pursuing an end which is morally unimportant (Peters, 1966a, p. 158). Even to a non-cricketer, however, this view seems to lack credibility. Suppose the argument were to be transferred from cricket to other self-justifying activities which are not in the business of truth-seeking: composing or performing a sonata, getting to know someone, making love, or performing religious rites. Is it really desirable that people with their priorities right should turn their backs on becoming a composer, pianist, friend, lover or worshipper and aim instead to be a student of creativity, personal relations, sex or religion? Or, given that social scientists can also engage personally in all these activities, is one to say that they ought to give, for example, the study of relationships priority over the development of friendship? There are things of value in the business of living beyond the illumination of life.

What is happening in the above paragraph is that the present writer is arguing with Peters about a (perhaps the ultimate) substantial value question. This seems a long way from the kind of philosophy demanded by the philosophical revolution outlined earlier in the chapter. Yet Peters seemed to be working within the new rules: did he not declare that the question 'What is your philosophy?' made the professional philosopher wince? It is clear, however, that underlying his arguments in defence of intellectual pursuits lies a vision of what constitutes the good life. We may or may not subscribe to this elevation of intellectual endeavour. We may wonder whether, because of the satisfaction derived from his academic career, Peters is projecting his own priorities in life as the universal ideal. What is beyond dispute, however, is that despite being a professional philosopher, R. S. Peters has a philosophy.

7

THE PHILOSOPHERS' CRITIQUE

Philosophical analysis can be carried out in different styles and for different purposes. As we have seen, it may aim to perform quite limited tasks like tidying up particular linguistic confusions. Perhaps this kind of operation could be conducted disinterestedly with the aim of achieving nothing beyond clarity. But there must always be scope for asking questions about why it is decided to analyse one bit of usage rather than another. Any answer would probably begin with the observation that the language chosen for analysis was particularly confused. But in addition it would seem likely that the philosopher viewed this area of discourse, and hence its clarification, as particularly important. The attention Austin gave to the analysis of promising doubtless reflected a view of moral philosophy and of morality itself in which the notion of 'promising' occupied a central position. Similarly, in philosophy of education, Ivan Snook's work on the concept of 'indoctrination' presumably sprang from a belief that it was crucially important to get clear about the difference between educating and indoctrinating (Snook, 1972).

But the choice of focal point may be determined by other considerations which are less compatible with a spirit of dispassionate neutrality. Where analysis is pursued in an aggressive style, the philosopher is in the business of choosing victims. It has already been shown how *Language, Truth and Logic* (Ayer, 1936) tried to dispose of God-talk by including the concept of 'God' in a large class of concepts which failed to measure up to new criteria of meaningfulness. But since 'God' is the central concept in most religions, religion itself was effectively being discredited. This shows that analytical philosophy and broader philosophizing are not so easily separated as some have supposed. For where analysis involves explaining things away, one's view of reality will determine what should be disposed of and what must be preserved.

Similar considerations influence philosophy of education. In this chapter we see Peters *et al.* in aggressive mood, performing demolition-by-analysis on particular concepts. The selection of concepts for scrutiny, however, is clearly not random, but determined by their central place in progressive educational theory. The desire to discredit child-centred education in this way has to be explained in terms of broader views of the kind which Peters has been shown to hold. As with the concept of 'God', hostile analysis of child-centred concepts was inspired by mistrust of the associated principles and practices.

This chapter deals with the critical treatment given by philosophers of education to the concepts of 'needs' and 'growth', and with their attempt to reinstate what they take to be the nature of knowledge as 'the heart of the educational process'. The bulk of the explicit criticism is to be found in three books: *The Philosophy of Primary Education* (1968) by R. F. Dearden, *Perspectives on Plowden* (1969) edited by R. S. Peters, and *A Critique of Current Educational Aims* edited by R. F. Dearden, P. H. Hirst and R. S. Peters (originally published in 1972 as the first part of *Education and the Development of Reason*, and appearing as a separate volume in 1975). But criticism of progressive educational theory also permeates the whole corpus of Peters, Hirst and Dearden.

The editors' introduction to *A Critique of Current Educational Aims* exhibits some of the hallmarks of recent philosophy of education. First, it is regretted that 'The statement and discussion of general aims is left to pundits, politicians and practical innovators who conduct it in an ambiguous and emotive manner' (Dearden *et al.*, 1975, p. ix). By implication, the papers in this volume are dispassionate and precise, the kind of virtues claimed for the professional academic as distinct from the interested amateur. Secondly, the mode of philosophizing is claimed to be that of general post-war philosophy. 'Most of these articles are, like most modern philosophy, analytic in their approach.' Finally, the introduction identifies the 'victim concepts': 'The authors in this collection are usually critical of attempts to characterise education in terms of "growth" or the satisfaction of "needs"' (*ibid.,*). The philosophers' analysis of 'needs' and 'growth' and their criticism of the use made of these concepts in child-centred writing will now be explored and assessed.

We noted in Chapter 1 that a characteristic observation in progressive educational theory is that the curriculum should be based on the child's needs and interests. Where there is a failure to match an educational programme to the needs of the learner, it is held that results will be unsatisfactory. Conversely there is a tendency to diagnose failure to profit from schooling in terms of lack of correspondence between pupils' needs and curriculum design. One 1960s curriculum paper, for example, observed:

> a frequent cause of failure seems to be that the course is often based on the traditional belief that there is a body of content for each separate subject which every school-leaver should know. In the least successful courses this body of knowledge is written into the curriculum without any real consideration of the needs of the boys and girls
>
> (Schools Council, 1967, p. 3)

While this kind of argument has a degree of plausibility, it would be unduly optimistic to suppose that a curriculum which was carefully geared to meeting pupils' needs would eliminate problems of pupil motivation. The relationship between need and motivation is not a sufficiently direct one. Even though I know that I *need* dental treatment, I may feel strongly tempted to cancel my appointment with the dentist if I have an aversion to that kind of experience. To get from existing needs to appropriate action can require strength of will and an ability to overrule disinclination in favour of long-term benefits. Clearly, however, young children cannot be expected to be motivated by very distant gains.

Dearden alleges that one of the attractions of trying to base educational practice on the needs of the child is the delusion that this 'will solve the problem of motivation' (Dearden, 1968, p. 17). Following much earlier analyses of the concept of 'need' by R. S. Peters (Peters, 1958; Benn and Peters, 1959), Dearden reaffirms the distinction between needs and wants, and suggests that these are confusedly equated by some child-centred theorists. Perhaps some may be guilty, but this is certainly not true of Rousseau's archetypal progressive writing which advises that the child be given 'not what he wants, but what he needs' (Rousseau, 1762, p. 49).

A further difficulty in basing a curriculum on children's needs is the problem of knowing who can tell what a child's educational needs are. At the beginning of *Primary Education in Scotland* we are told: 'The suggestions now being made are based on what is known of the growth and development of the child, and emphasis is laid on the importance of fashioning the curriculum according to his needs at the various stages of his development' (SED, 1965, p. viii). This suggests that for the identification of needs progressivism is likely to turn to developmental psychology. Dearden complains that the listing of these needs appears in a part of the Memorandum devoted to psychology (Dearden, 1968, p. 14). The process of identifying needs could therefore be portrayed as a scientific operation, and hence seen as a convenient way both of sidestepping value questions about aims, and of endowing a preferred approach to education with the authority of science. A need, however, is not a property that can be observed or established simply by empirical methods: yet it is easy to slip into this mode of thought. One account of child-centred thinking, for example, explains it in these terms: 'The primary function of schools was to attend to the needs and interests of pupils: these, and other *character-istics of learners themselves*, were assumed to be the principal determinants of the curriculum' (Kirk, 1982, p. 35, emphasis added).

It is worth remembering here that the identification of a need does not always require an expert. We all know that if people are starving they need food. But it is true that we often expect scientists, including psychologists and doctors, to tell us what we need. Suppose a scientist insists that we all need fresh air, exercise, and vitamin X. The natural question to ask is 'What do we need these things *for*?' If the answer is 'To prevent premature senility and disintegration of the knees', we shall readily agree that fresh air, exercise and vitamin X are among our needs. Just as it is better to have some food than to starve to death, it is obviously very undesirable to have knees or minds that refuse to function.

In education, however, there is likely to be disagreement about what it is to enjoy educational health or to be educationally well nourished. Another way of putting the same point is to say that there appears to be no consensus about the kind of person we want education to produce: some people, for example, will demand that schools foster the acceptance of conventional social norms, others will emphasize the encouragement of pupils to develop independence of mind. Thus, identification of educational needs cannot proceed independently of a consideration of educational aims and values. What, after all, is the difference between claiming (as the Primary Memorandum does) that children have a need for understanding, and asserting (as the Primary Memorandum also does) that in education the promotion of understanding is a fundamental aim? Disagreements about aims, however, clearly reflect differences over values. As Dearden puts it, 'One has to look behind statements of need to the values that are guiding them, for it is here that the issue substantially lies' (Dearden, 1968, p. 16). And once this move is made, we have moved beyond the field where we can appeal to psychologists for a scientific judgement.

Perhaps, however, Dearden's most serious charge is that talk of a needs-based curriculum is ultimately vacuous because it offers no basis for judging one kind of curriculum to be preferable to another. Where a vocationally oriented curriculum is favoured, it can be said that the development of such a curriculum is justified by the pupil's need to be financially self-supporting. If one advocates a curriculum which gives priority to the promotion of spiritual development, then one is claiming that spiritual development is the child's overriding need. If any curriculum can be construed or defended as a needs-based curriculum, it might indeed seem that the injunction to base the curriculum on the needs of the child offers no positive guidance.

There are two possible ways this charge might be met. It might be argued that 'need' points to something fairly basic, and that many things that are educationally valuable are not in this category. What, it might be asked, is a knowledge of Shakespeare necessary *for*? The assumption in such an argument is that a needs-based curriculum should be understood to mean providing learners with essential skills – a kind of personal survival kit. While this is at least meaningful in the sense that it excludes a range of learning that makes no useful contribution to such an end, it is not the kind of curriculum that appeals to many progressives, who are more likely to stress the importance of schools catering for the child's need for self-expression and independent discovery.

The other possible response to the charge of vacuousness is to shift the emphasis from the *needs* of the child to the needs of the *child,* and to stress that children's needs must be given priority over the needs of industry (or of the state, the party, the church or whatever). In a convenient world, of course, there might be no conflict between these different aims. However, one has to allow for the possibility (and surely it is more than a possibility) that sometimes one of these aims will have to be given priority over the others. The progressive view is that the needs of the individual child must come first. This position is seen as stemming from a moral commitment to the children for whom the educator is responsible. A pupil ought to be respected as a person, not for his or her potential as a future contributor to the national economy, or as a future servant of the church or party. But further, the insistence on attending to the child's needs involves a reaffirmation of the importance of making education 'harmonize' with the existing nature of individual children. Not to take account of this would be to show scant respect for the person that the child already is.

Dearden's analysis of 'needs' in education seems a very useful exercise. But it is one thing to see his points as illuminating the nature of the concept, and quite another to decide what follows from this. Following his argument that 'every curriculum is a needs-curriculum', he advises 'giving up talk about a curriculum based on children's needs'. Certainly, without some further specification, this notion seems alarmingly elastic. But it would be perverse to abandon a concept altogether when we have just been provided with an improved understanding of it. It should now be possible to appreciate what we are doing when we appeal to the concept of 'need': potentially, therefore it becomes *more* useful rather than less. Its usefulness seems not to be lost on Peters himself when he writes in the preface to *Perspectives on Plowden*: 'we are very strongly of the opinion that views based on a wider and more exact knowledge of relevant research and a clearer understanding of *the distinctive needs* of the present and immediate future are now needed' (Peters, 1969, p. ix, emphasis added).

The identity of these 'needs of the present and immediate future' is not revealed – indeed it is unclear whether Peters is talking about the needs of the primary school or of educational theory or of something else. Are these needs supposed to be immediately evident to any observer? Or is it being suggested that such needs can be ascertained through understanding or perhaps through 'relevant research'? Yet the point made by Dearden about the needs of children applies equally here: the needs of the present depend directly on what one believes the present ought to be like. At bottom, a needs statement assumes a value judgement.

This point in Dearden's analysis seems a particularly useful one. A heightened awareness of the goal-directed character of needs statements might have produced a better account of the child's needs in the Primary Memorandum. These are said to be:

- the need for security,
- the need for guidance,
- the need for freedom,
- the need to understand, and
- the need for the 'real' and the 'concrete'.

It is, however, surely important to consider whether the 'need for security' and the 'need for the "real" and the "concrete"' require fulfilment for the realization of different goals: in the former case, perhaps for some desirable type of affective development, and in the latter case, for learning and understanding. Yet 'understanding' is itself listed as one of the five needs of the child. It seems that these needs exist at different levels. Understanding is an educational goal, while the 'real' and the 'concrete' are means to achieving that goal. Here, surely, we have an illustration of how an analysis of the concept of 'need' could lead, not to the abandonment of the notion, but to a more rational and systematic approach to delineating the needs of children.

There is no reason why the child-centred educationist should not accept Dearden's lesson: the valuational character of needs statements should certainly be recognized and made explicit. What concerns Dearden is that instead of this happening the concept of need is invoked as a comfortable substitute for aims and values.

Is this allegation fair? Dearden's illustration is the Primary Memorandum, 'the first chapter of which is not, as one might reasonably have expected it to be, devoted to setting out aims, but rather gives a statement of "the needs of the child"' (Dearden, 1968, p. 14). Many teachers and trainee teachers will have read this critical observation in *The Philosophy of Primary Education* and assumed it to be accurate. Inspection of the relevant section of the Memorandum, however, shows that, whatever may be thought of the *quality* of the argument, the *form* of the argument is perfectly reasonable. First, aims are clearly, if very generally, stated, and only then does the report proceed to identify needs which must be met if these aims are to be realized. The Primary Memorandum, a document which has played a crucial part in the development of child-centred education in Scotland, is therefore not guilty of using needs statements to bypass discussion of aims. The evidence for its acquittal appears in the first paragraph of the section on needs where the report talks of producing 'citizens who are skilful, knowledgeable, adaptable, capable of co-operation, and as far as possible of leadership'. And it concludes:

The function of the primary school, therefore, is not merely to prepare him [the child] for secondary education or to teach him the basic skills, but to begin to prepare him for life. Consequently it must concern itself with the whole child, fashioning its organisation, its curriculum and its methods in such a way as to cater for every facet of his developing personality. The needs of the child which the primary school must try to meet if it is to accomplish this challenging and complex task are set out below.

(SED, 1965, p. 11)

Then follows the list of needs which we have already noted, accompanied by the committee's comments.

Perhaps, of course, 'The child needs security' could just as well have been written in the form 'The teacher ought to provide security for the child, otherwise the child will not be able to develop in accordance with our specified educational aims.' As has been suggested elsewhere (Woodhead, 1987), needs statements may be seen as a kind of shorthand. Aims-statements about preparing children for life are too general and distant to be useful for guiding classroom practice. In enumerating five needs, the Memorandum has derived from this kind of aims statement a short list of reminders of what teachers could and should do to contribute towards the realization of such an aim. Conceptualizing these points in terms of 'the needs of the child' is a graphic way of underlining the obligation that teachers are under to attend to these important matters. We can use this idea to interpret the Plowden Report's chapter on 'The aims of primary education' where we read: 'Children *need* to be themselves, to live with other children and with grown ups, to learn from their environment, to enjoy the present, to get ready for the future, to create and to love, to learn to face adversity, to behave responsibly, in a word, to be human beings' (CACE, 1967, p. 188, emphasis added). Here the idea of producing human beings is too general to be helpful: the list of the child's needs is intended to point to the important features of a human being (as understood by the Committee) which should be given particular attention.

Further, in elaborating on its own list of needs, the Primary Memorandum shows no sign of value avoidance. For example, the child is said to have a need for guidance 'in order that his emotional, moral and social development may follow a pattern which will make him acceptable to the society in which he will live as an adult' (SED, 1965, p. 12). One of the desirable outcomes of meeting the child's need for freedom is made equally clear: 'His ability to express himself and to communicate with others can only be hampered by the imposition in the classroom of an unnatural silence' (*ibid.*, p. 13). A needs statement is thus a convenient and effective way of indicating the kind of educational experience it is important for children to undergo. We can legitimately express such judgments in this form provided we neither forget nor conceal the nature of needs statements. Contrary to the spirit of Dearden's writing, his critical points can be viewed as elucidating a concept rather than as exterminating it.

If we turn now to the criticism levelled by Peters and Dearden at the use made of concepts of 'growth' and 'development' in child-centred writing, we find some of the same critical points reappearing: 'Talk of "development", like talk of children's "needs", is too often a way of dressing up our value-judgments in semi-scientific clothes' (Peters, 1969, p. 8). What form does this talk take? One influential metaphor which pervades what Dearden has called 'the European tradition' of child-centred theorizing likens education to horticulture, the teacher to a gardener, and the pupil to a growing plant.

The classic statement of the horticulture analogy is to be found in Pestalozzi's *Address to My House, 1818*. The true type of education, Pestalozzi says:

> is like the art of the gardener under whose care a thousand trees blossom and grow. He contributes nothing to their actual growth: the principle of growth lies in the trees themselves. He plants and waters, but God gives the increase. It is not the gardener who opens the roots of the trees that they may draw food from the earth; it is not he who divides the pith from the wood and the wood from the bark, and thus helps forward the development of the separate parts . . . . Of all this he does nothing; he only waters the dry earth that the roots may not strike it as a stone. He only drains away the standing water that the tree may not suffer . . . . So with the educator: he imparts no single power to man. He gives neither life nor breath. He only watches lest any external force should injure or disturb. He takes care that development runs its course in accordance with its own laws . . . . He knows that sound methods of popular education must agree with the external laws according to which these powers unfold.
>
> (Green, 1912, p. 195)

What are held to be the implications of this growth metaphor for teaching?

(1) Teachers are not absolutely essential. Children can and do grow intellectually as well as physically without close and continuous professional supervision. Plants and children are alike in that both can achieve maturity without outside intervention: in certain conditions, wild flowers and fruit will flourish, often appearing more beautiful or delicious than the carefully cultivated kind. If this seems to imply an educational policy of indifference and carelessness, it had better be recalled that Pestalozzi says that the model educator 'watches lest any external force should injure or disturb', while Froebel claims that education is a matter of 'guarding and protecting' (Froebel, 1826, p. 7).

(2) Children, like plants, go through different stages of development. If teachers are to help children to mature, they must have a sound

understanding of children's nature and their developmental stages. A corollary of the importance attached to this knowledge is the view that those who do not have it may actually harm children if they intervene in their development.

(3) There are limits to what teaching can achieve. Teachers are not responsible for creating an end-product. Rather they accept the nature of the child, and assist and enrich development that takes place independently of any teacher's endeavours. This philosophy of teaching is fortified first by an optimistic view of human nature (manifest, for example, in Roussseau's opposition to the doctrine of original sin), and second by the equally optimistic view that free development will be for the best. In Froebel, this belief is, as we would expect, set in the context of theistic metaphysics:

> the undisturbed operation of the Divine Unity is necessarily good – can not be otherwise than good. This necessity implies that the young human being – as it were, still in process of creation – would seek, although still unconsciously, as a product of nature, yet decidedly and surely, that which is in itself best; and moreover, in a form wholly adapted to his condition, as well as to his disposition, his powers and means.
>
> (Froebel, 1826, pp. 7–8)

One particular limitation which teachers should note is that they cannot force the pace of children's development. Any attempt to do so will, at best, be unsatisfactory. Rousseau is explicit on this point: 'Nature would have them children before they are men. If we try to invert this order we shall produce a forced fruit immature and flavourless, fruit which will be rotten before it is ripe' (Rousseau, 1762, p. 54); 'Leave childhood to ripen in children' (*ibid.*, p. 58).

(4) What teachers can contribute to the child's development cannot be achieved through domination and command. What they do has to be done indirectly by ensuring, as far as possible, optimal conditions for growth. The horticulture analogy again serves to remind us that even this kind of contribution knows limits. While some conditions encourage healthy growth, others make it unlikely: but although gardeners can feed the soil, or turn up the temperature in the greenhouse, they cannot control the weather.

Dearden levels three main points of criticism at this portrayal of the educational process: it is too individualistic (1968, p. 33); it is deterministic (1972, p. 66); and it is vague (1968, p. 34). In themselves, these criticisms seem to have some substance; and they will be restated and redeveloped here.

(1) The horticultural metaphor is too individualistic. Children interact with parents, with teachers and with each other: only the most eccentric gardeners, however, converse with their plants. That chil-

dren are social beings should not be seen as one of the many interesting but contingent facts which, if borne in mind, will promote better teaching: it is, rather, something quite fundamental. But for the interaction of the child with others, education could not begin. If this point seems obvious, it does no harm to recall that it was not always so. There is a story that King James VI of Scotland – an experimental psychologist before his time – sent an infant (and a deaf mute nurse) to an uninhabited island to test the hypothesis that, removed from contaminating contact with the local tongue, people would 'naturally' acquire God's language, that is Hebrew. Unsurprisingly, no language was acquired. The charge of individualism, however, cannot be levelled at all educationists who make 'growth' a central concept: it would certainly not apply to Dewey's philosophy (which will be the subject of a separate comment below).

(2) The metaphor is deterministic. It suggests that the child's growth can be wholly explained in terms of an interaction between inner mechanisms and external conditions and forces. But a child's educational development cannot be accounted for in these crude terms of cause and effect. Children's reactions are often unpredictable. They have active, independent and increasingly rational powers of judgement. Their understanding of the world, and their perception of their own possible futures within it affect the way they develop. Children can take an active part in their own education They may choose to devote their energies to interests which are at odds with the priorities of their schools; or they can decide to ignore, resist, or mock the efforts of their teachers. Plants, however, cannot outwit gardeners. In so far as a mechanistic account of educational development excludes the notion of the child-as-agent, it is belittling and offensive. Again, while some educationists envisage a predetermined pattern of development, Dewey conceives of an essentially fluid style of social interaction with open-ended outcomes.

(3) The metaphor is vague. While appearing to illuminate the nature of education, the metaphor obscures difficulties in providing an adequate characterization, for it fails to provide criteria for what is to count as a desirable manifestation of growth. What constitutes a fine marrow or carnation is not too difficult to settle, but people have always argued over what it is to be an educated person, or a mature, fully realized human being.

This weakness in the growth metaphor can be illustrated from an exposition of the philosophy of Bedales, one of the earliest of the English independent progressive schools, written by its third headmaster, H. B. Jacks:

> You begin with the child and you recognize that, because he is what he is, a person in his own right, a human being, he has certain

qualities, abilities, interests, potentialities that have got to grow, and that it is your business to help them to do so, to give them now the kind of food they need, and to protect them from things like overfeeding, malnutrition and atrophy. Imagination, inquisitiveness, awareness, sensitivity, creative skill – not all of them, of course, in equal proportions in every individual; there will be more of them in some, less in others, with no two individuals exactly the same. Yet each of us is, as a German thinker put it, 'A unique experiment in the eyes of God', and each of us is capable of growth within the limitations of his own natural endowments, provided the nourishment is there. The more standardised, organised, systematised education becomes, and the more subservient it is to those outside pressures which we call 'the demands of modern life' – pressures which today are relentless and terrific – the less likely it is to satisfy the needs of the individuals it deals with.

(Jacks, 1962, p. 38–9)

Jacks goes on to ask: 'What are the requirements to make this possible? A boarding school, with . . . both sexes together; true growth is impossible with so unnatural an arrangement as the segregation of the sexes' (*ibid.*, pp. 38–9).

Jacks' appeal to the notion of growth serves to fortify resistance to forms of education which he finds unacceptable. It is implied that education should not be standardized, organized or systematized, and that it should not be determined by outside pressures. But what *positive* indication can the concept of 'growth' give of the form which education *should* take? Is *any* kind of growth acceptable? In the second part of the extract it is significant that the writer has to introduce – apparently without noticing – a notion of 'true growth' to distinguish between the kind of growth he thinks desirable, and growth which is not. 'True growth,' he says, 'is impossible in single-sex schools.' Since, however, it is obvious that children in single-sex schools do grow and develop, the reader is left wondering what Jacks' criteria are for distinguishing between growth which is 'true' and growth which is not. One might speculate that Jacks means that in a boys' school pupils do not grow properly because they come to view girls as sex objects, or perhaps idealize them as ineffably pure. But if the writer thinks that education should promote certain attitudes to the opposite sex, he should say as much, specifying what these preferred attitudes are, and explaining on what grounds they are deemed desirable.

What this seems to show is that while the growth metaphor clearly rules out certain pedagogical strategies – for example, trying to accelerate cognitive development – it provides inadequate positive guidance on its own. To make up for this limitation, further value judgements must be made.

The same conclusion seems to emerge from an examination of Dewey's conception of education as a process of growth. As we saw in Chapter 3, Dewey clarifies his own notion of growth by contrasting it with Froebel's.

Froebel is said to have seen education as a way of assisting a fixed programme of development towards a pre-ordained end. For Dewey, however, growth was not to be valued because it led to some end-state: it was something of inherent value. But not all kinds of growth were of equal value: according to Dewey, growth is valuable to the extent to which it facilitates or promotes further growth.

Dearden takes as his target here a notorious weak point in Dewey's account: he raises the difficulty that in committing an antisocial act like robbing a bank, a gang of criminals may be furthering their development and enriching their own experience (Dearden, 1972, p. 78). Dewey, who was aware of this kind of objection, argued that this kind of activity actually limited the agents' growth since it cut them off from social intercourse. This argument only works, however, if the enrichment derived from wealth falls short of the benefits of interacting freely without the disadvantages of having to conceal one's criminal activities.

Essentially Dearden is right. The portrayal of education as a process of growth rules out directive teaching but falls short of providing positive alternative guidance about what forms of growth are desirable. For this it must be supplemented by value judgements – at the very least by declarations that antisocial behaviour is unacceptable. The growth metaphor has been expected to do too much on its own.

Dearden concedes that analogies are not identities (Dearden, 1968, p. 49); but it would seem reasonable to conclude from this that any metaphor, however apt and illuminating, can mislead if it is understood too literally. David Aspin has suggested that a metaphor is a kind of 'persuasive definition': it is designed to encourage us to look at something familiar in a new light (Aspin, 1984, p. 33). This can only happen, of course, if the hearer or reader is prepared to respond: perhaps people vary in their willingness to enter into such imaginative games. The term 'game' is used here to indicate not just the need for more than one participant, but as a reminder that generating a metaphor is an inspired move for producing new (but partial) illumination: it does not lay solemn claim to stating the whole truth. It has been argued that metaphors are at their most powerful when they are new, when they have 'the capacity to startle and disturb' (Elliott, 1984, p. 40). But a persuasive definition can also exert influence, quietly and unobtrusively, by becoming part of our established intellectual framework, something that we absorb without even recognizing that the idea has been adopted.

If nothing else, Dearden has done a service in alerting us to the pervasiveness of the concept of growth in educational writing. Once the assumption-laden nature of this kind of talk has been identified, then it can be unpacked and scrutinized, and subsequently endorsed or rejected. But on what basis? The value of any metaphor is surely to be assessed in terms of the positive illumination it offers rather than in terms of its limitations. The focus of the philosophers' critique, however, has been on the ways in which the analogy fails. But if pointing to limitations were to be allowed to discredit metaphors, then they would all have to go.

Of course it is useful to be reminded of the limitations of one's own preferred metaphors. There is no reason why philosophers of education should not elucidate the growth metaphor's shortcomings and at the same time view it sympathetically as a valuable source of insight. Pestalozzi himself was well aware that the analogy he drew was only partial:

> the human organism differs from inanimate objects: it differs too from animals and plants . . . . The tree is subject to the influences of inanimate Nature against which its vital powers can offer no resistance, whereas the higher spirit which dwells in man is free to allow his sensory nature and sensory environment to bring about his ruin, or to work against and overcome them.
>
> (Green, 1912, pp. 190–1)

Peters, however, saw the philosophical treatment given to the growth metaphor as fatal: 'it cannot remain for long romantically aloft once the glare of philosophical analysis is turned upon it' (Peters, 1963, p. 94). I have argued that this analysis elucidates the concept of growth. Peters believes the analysis discredits it. One way of explaining these different reactions is to suggest that Peters' dismissal of the growth metaphor stems not from its perceived inadequacies, but from his own broader philosophy of education. The logical gap between analysis and rejection is crossed by a leap, not of faith, but of concern.

Peters and Dearden are opposed to any model of education which seems to reduce the role of the teacher or which rules out the deliberate acceleration of the learning process. This is evident from the fact that Peters emblazons a statement of B. F. Skinner's on the frontispiece of *Perspectives on Plowden*: ' The school of experience is no school at all, not because no one learns in it but because no one teaches. Teaching is the expedition of learning; a person who is taught learns more quickly than one who is not' (Peters, 1969, p. iii). Here we have a revealing contrast with the traditional progressive suspicion, from Rousseau onwards, of fast learning: as we have seen, 'real', non-superficial learning, is often held to be best achieved slowly through experience.

The influence of practical concerns about teaching and learning at this point is entirely proper. What is important, however, is that it should be made explicit that the metaphor's critics, far from being disinterested and dispassionate practitioners of philosophical analysis, are, just like the metaphor's exponents, observers of the educational scene who want certain things to happen, or stop happening, in schools. Those committed to the growth metaphor are concerned to highlight, through it, what they see as the perversities of traditional educational practice, while opposition to the metaphor reflects a more conservative approach to schooling. People's view of the metaphor's worth is thus a reflection of their educational values.

To be fair, however, it has to be said that the critics' opposition to growth theory is often moderate and qualified. It is commonly suggested that: (i) it was appropriate and useful to state the case for education as growth at the time when school was authoritarian and narrowly academic; (ii) this time has now passed – education is now conducted along enlightened and liberal lines; and consequently (iii) the continued labouring of the growth metaphor is unhelpful and possibly dangerous. Thus, for example, R. S. Peters: 'It was understandable about forty years ago that reformers should proclaim that "education is growth" or that children should be encouraged to learn from experience; for there was a great deal wrong, both morally and psychologically, with the old elementary school tradition' (Peters, 1969, p. 1). And R. F. Dearden writes: 'What the growth theory has always done is at least to stress the side of that ideal balance which has typically been understressed in the more authoritarian kind of education which until quite recently was traditional' (Dearden, 1972, p. 81). The strategy here seems to be to portray growth theory as having historical importance, but historical importance *only*. It was developed, so it is suggested, as a critique of certain forms of education; and now that these are no longer in evidence, the theory is irrelevant. Thus, behind the philosophers' rejection of growth theory lies the view that current educational practice was already sufficiently liberated from the old ways. This view of education explains Peters' desire to expose the concept of growth to 'the glare of philosophical analysis'. Yet the implicit suggestion that such an investigation will proceed dispassionately sits ill with the habit Peters shares with Dearden of referring to the metaphor and its associated ideas as 'growth doctrine', or more commonly (and worse) 'growth ideology'.

As with the previous victim concept, there remains a question to be raised about how far the critical points actually apply to contemporary statements of child-centred education. The interest shown in the growth of the child by the Plowden Report and the Primary Memorandum reflects a belief in the importance of educational psychology as the key to determining the optimal educational programme. Part Two of the Plowden Report may be called 'The Growth of the Child': it is not, however, an attempt to characterize the nature of the educational process, but is a review of relevant evidence. According to Plowden, 'Knowledge of the manner in which children develop . . . is of prime importance, both in avoiding educationally harmful practices and in introducing effective ones. In the last 50 years much work has been done on the physical, emotional and intellectual growth of children' (CACE, 1967, p. 7). Similarly, the Primary Memorandum was seen by its authors as being 'built around Piaget' (Farquharson, 1985). In crude terms we may say that for the two reports, growth is an important datum, while for Froebel and Dewey it represents a goal.

Of course one can never absolutely discount the influence of a powerful metaphor. Perhaps its effect can be seen in the Plowden Report's talk of 'conditions which nourish, as it were, intellectual and emotional growth'. But in neither report is there any appeal to the idea of an unfolding plant as a way of illuminating the nature of the educational process. So even if the philosophers' criticisms of the horticultural metaphor are more damaging than has been suggested here, they would not seem to discredit contemporary statements of child-centred educational theory.

The critique of the concepts of 'needs' and 'growth' is essentially a ground-clearing exercise to allow an alternative to child-centred education to be advanced. The difference in the position advanced by the philosophers can be seen most clearly at the curriculum level.

How the child-centred educationist thinks about the curriculum can be indicated through a number of key passages from the Primary Memorandum and the Plowden Report:

- The acquisition of knowledge and skills, once the main aim of education, is no longer as important as it was . . . . Much more vital today . . . are the fostering of intellectual curiosity, and the development of the capacity to acquire knowledge independently.

  (SED, 1965, p. 18)

- Primary education . . . will have failed the age and society it serves if children leave the primary school without the right attitude to learning.

  (*ibid.*, p.37)

- Many of the activities which are recommended involve elements of more than one 'subject', and serve to advance the pupils' knowledge and skill in more than one field . . . . 'Integration' of this kind should be a feature of primary education at all stages.

  (*ibid.*, p. 37).

- knowledge does not fall into neatly separate compartments . . . work and play are not opposite but complementary.

  (CACE, 1967, p. 187)

Such observations show that in their thinking about the curriculum child-centred educationists advocate some form of curriculum integration and attach great importance to the maintenance of interest in children. These two ideas are often seen as interrelated: children's drive to find out about the world leads their minds to range widely; the kind of question they are interested in recognizes no subject boundary. It is sometimes further suggested that the differences between traditional divisions of knowledge have been overdrawn: the techniques involved in these disciplines need to be demystified and seen as minor variations of a general skill of enquiry.

In the writing of philosophers of education very different kinds of emphasis are presented. In his inaugural lecture and elsewhere, Peters argues that education is a process of 'initiation' involving 'experienced persons turning the eye of others outwards to what is essentially independent of persons' (Peters, 1966a, p. 54). This independent sphere consists of 'differentiated modes of thought and awareness' which are said to be independent and radically different in kind, even though, for example, those working in the scientific mode may make use of mathematical knowledge (Hirst and Peters, 1970, p. 65).

This idea was developed by Hirst along lines that have proved remarkably influential. 'Detailed studies', it was declared 'suggest that some seven areas can be distinguished' (Hirst and Peters, 1970, p. 63). In his much reprinted essay 'Liberal education and the nature of knowledge' (1965), mention is made of the following: mathematics, physical science, human science, history, religion, literature and the fine arts, and philosophy. In The *Logic of Education*, although seven areas are again referred to, careful reading reveals that they are not the same seven. History and human science have disappeared to be replaced by 'moral judgement and awareness' and 'awareness and understanding of our own and other people's minds'. With two apparently different lists being produced, one wonders about the criteria on which these classifications are based, and about how much reliance can be placed on them.

Hirst's preference for talking about forms (and subforms) of *knowledge* raised particular difficulties about whether literature, for example, could properly be included under such a rubric: Hirst's determination to argue that the fine arts constituted a form of knowledge prompted the charge that he suffered from 'an incorrigible need to square circles' (Wilson, 1977).

Peters represents knowledge as essentially a series of craft activities, each with its own standards and ways of proceeding. Certainly there would seem little profit in an apprenticeship scheme which failed to recognize the differences between carpentry and pottery (even if a lathe appears to operate somewhat like a potter's wheel). A novice would have to be shown that each had its own mode of operation. To extend the trades analogy along lines in keeping with Hirst's intentions, plumbing works on very different principles from electrical systems: but central-heating engineers have to draw on the skills of a trained electrician before the installation can be completed.

To talk in these terms is to present a picture in which different activities are not at odds with each other: rather, they complement each other. For some of the forms which Peters and Hirst depict, however, coexistence is far from typical. Religion and science have very commonly been at loggerheads because they do not confine themselves to the exploration of separate concerns. They can equally well be seen as alternative ways of understanding the same phenomena: by its very nature, religion is inclined to generate this kind of overarching interpretation of life itself. The point of having 'church' or 'denominational' schools is presumably that such institutions are enabled to propagate a distinctively religious view of the universe and man's place in it. It is perhaps on the question of human nature that conflict of this kind is most obvious: we have already noted Rousseau's attempt to displace the concept of 'original sin' by advancing what can be seen as a scientific hypothesis that undesirable character traits can be explained in terms of the impact of social factors. The scientific mode of thought is not readily confined to the laboratory: its admirers tend to advocate its application in an ever-increasing range of contexts where its credentials will inevitably be challenged. Intellectual conflict of this kind is an inescapable part of our culture.

While its inability to accommodate such conflict may render the Peters/ Hirst model of knowledge suspect, its emphasis on divisions within knowledge has earned it a favourable hearing among those in schools who are unsympathetic to 'curriculum integration'. An integrated curriculum is not normally one which has as its primary aim that of making children aware of the different structures of the different forms – though one wonders why, if the differences are indeed so radical, it is necessary to be preoccupied with asserting what should be obvious. While a differentiated knowledge could theoretically be transmitted through an integrated curriculum, Peters and Hirst discourage teachers from attempting this by observing that 'project and topic work can only too easily degenerate into pursuits which, *however interesting*, have little or no educational value' (Hirst and Peters, 1970, p. 71, emphasis added). But of course the force of this warning depends on one's acceptance of the philosophers' touchstone for educational value: in Peters' terms, education is the process of being initiated into different forms of thought.

Since this prescriptive criterion is seen as a matter of logic, it ought to be applicable to any educational enterprise, regardless of context or of any teaching tradition, as can be seen from the following discussion of nursery education:

> in a well-run nursery children are safe and their health is looked after . . . there are many opportunities to work out personal difficulties and to achieve some sort of balanced emotional development . . . children learn to talk to each other freely, to share, co-operate, help others and so on. Above all, it might be said, a child who goes to a nursery has a greater chance of being secure and happy. But while each of these things that have just been mentioned is very important, and nothing that I shall say will minimize its importance, it is not education . . . .
>
> For the play activities which are arranged in a nursery, or indeed in an infant school, to be regarded as specifically educational, and not just useful, therapeutic, or happiness-producing, it would have to be shown that they are continuous with the development of the kind of *differentiated understanding* which has been referred to as giving 'cognitive perspective' to one's experience. And since it is no accident that such a development is what is to be sought during the more formal schooling which follows the nursery stage, we can say

that if the activities of the nursery are to be regarded as educational, then they must be continuous with what is to be sought in later schooling, and not just arranged with an eye to health and safe amusement.

(Dearden, 1967, pp. 88–9, emphasis added)

First, on the contrast drawn between education and 'safe amusement' it will be enough to note that this indicates (as does the previous quotation from Hirst and Peters) the philosophers' relative disregard of 'interestingness' as a mark of the educationally valuable. Children's interests seem to be viewed by Dearden with some suspicion apparently because they may be acquired in environments which are 'culturally deprived'. Even to *start* from the existing interests of such children, according to Dearden, would be to 'trivialise the curriculum' (Dearden, 1968, p. 22).

Second, whatever the intentions of the observations on nursery education, these could clearly be seen as having implications of a kind not normally associated with the tidying up of concepts. The professional standing of people who work in nursery schools depends heavily on being seen as educators and members of the teaching profession.

Third, Dearden's argument about what counts as an educational activity would be equally applicable to what children do at home. Their play, their interests and their experiences would have to be judged as educationally valuable only if they were 'continuous with' the development of a differentiated understanding. To invoke the traditional school's model of knowledge in this context, however, would seem quite inappropriate: on such a criterion, the only parents who further their children's education would probably be those who assist with their homework. This dismissal of so much that is of educational benefit to the child is surely a *reductio ad absurdum* of the philosophers' conception of education.

Despite his lack of sympathy for most aspects of child-centred thinking about the curriculum, Dearden detects one fragment of value which he declares to be 'personal autonomy based on reason' (Dearden, 1968, p. 46). However, for these philosophers of education, reason is identified with mathematics, science, and other forms of knowledge. When the Primary Memorandum (SED, 1965) stresses 'the development of the capacity to acquire knowledge independently', Dearden would be happy to endorse such a view provided it was understood as pointing to a differentiated curriculum rather than, as the Memorandum suggests, an integrated curriculum. Ironically, child-centred educationists here end up being put into a situation where they can be recognized by philosophers as making a worthwhile point provided they accept that their contribution implies just the kind of curriculum that many of them want to reject.

As a final criticism of the philosophers' challenge to the child-centred curriculum let me point to the logical gulf which exists between Hirst's account of knowledge and the recommendations that are derived from it. Interestingly, the seeds of this criticism are to be found in something

Dearden says about the defects of the Plowden Report's famous argument about the centrality of the child: 'No advances in policy, no acquisitions of new equipment, have their desired effect unless they are in harmony with the nature of the child, unless they are fundamentally acceptable to him' (CACE, 1967, p. 7). Dearden goes on to observe:

> This sheer assertion, which is in no way derivable from the empirical research in which it is embedded, is in reality a major policy statement. Yet it assumes: (i) that the child has a 'nature', which is a dubious metaphysical assertion; (ii) that we ought to adopt the principle of always starting from and being acceptable to this 'nature', which is an unargued ethical recommendation.
>
> (Dearden, 1969, p. 24)

Yet the philosophers' own recommendations about the curriculum are open to exactly the same kind of objections. Suppose Hirst's portrayal of knowledge can be deemed sound. Does anything follow from this about how knowledge should be presented to children? No one can claim that educators should give primary consideration to the nature of knowledge and at the same time reject the Plowden dictum for the reasons given by Dearden. For Dearden's criticisms, suitably transposed, apply with equal force to Hirst's position, as can be seen if we paraphrase Plowden's observation above: 'At the heart of the educational process lie the forms of knowledge. No developments in teaching or in curriculum design will prove satisfactory unless they are in harmony with the nature of the forms and correspond to their demands.' If Plowden is guilty of assertion and unargued recommendation, so too are the philosophers.

Perhaps the earliest child-centred educationist to claim that a revolution was in progress was John Dewey. In this revolution, as we saw in Chapter 3, the child was to become the centre round which would be organized the teacher, the textbook, and everything else. For Hirst, however, the organizing principles of education seem to be determined by a particular view of the nature of knowledge rather than by the nature of the child. Philosophers of education are therefore not spectators at the revolution, but counter-revolutionaries.

8

THE POWER OF PETERS

This book started by examining the Utopian story of Emile, often seen as offering an impractical version of progressive education. While the book's publication created vast interest, its principles were at the time tried out only on a very small scale. It was this failure to transform educational practice that led Pestalozzi to declare in 1826: '*Emile* . . . est resté . . . un livre fermé.' The 1960s and 1970s, however, offer a remarkable contrast. Child-centred education had made significant inroads into the practice of teaching: it was no longer seen as Utopian.

But now, as will be documented in Chapters 9 and 10, another major change is under way in primary schools. As we approach the end of the century, child-centred education is under pressure. The roots of this change go back a long way. Malcolm Skilbeck has identified the mid-1970s as the point when Hirst's thinking was adopted by the Inspectorate in England and Wales (Skilbeck, 1984, p. 33). Hirst's writing on forms of knowledge was continually used to sustain a subject-divided curriculum. In the early 1980s Scotland's educational establishment began to show signs of wavering from its commitment to child-centred thinking for the first time since 1965. In *Primary Education in the Eighties* the Committee on Primary Education cited Dearden's account of the 'forms of understanding' as a basis for its deliberations on the curriculum; and it noted that the Memorandum's use of concepts like 'growth' and 'needs' had been 'rigorously and critically examined' by Dearden. These concepts made only one further appearance in the document, and that in an account of progressivism's historical development where they appear in quotation marks, presumably to indicate their dubious validity: 'The child's "needs" were to be put at the centre of the teaching process and his educational "growth" controlled by his own physical and mental development' (COPE, 1983, p. 24). Why were the makers of policy so impressed by writing from a discipline which could easily have been dismissed as mere theory? Part of the answer is that this new philosophy of education was written deliberately to be seen as of practical relevance to schools. Rousseau wrote imaginatively, and subversively, about children and learning in a way which shunned educational institutions and which drew no distinction between education and child-rearing. Peters and his colleagues, by contrast, knew that their audience was not the general reading public, but the teacher and the student teacher; and the field of enquiry was therefore focused on the institutions of which these readers had firsthand experience.

It is significant that while there was some philosophical treatment of higher education during the Peters period, there was no philosophy of the earliest stage of education: one-year-olds do not attend educational institutions, and their principal educators are not professional teachers who attend lecture courses on education. As deschoolers have pointed out, in the public mind education has become identified with schools: it is disturbing when philosophy of education itself becomes trapped into this view by having a school-oriented audience. Peters and Dearden are content to operate within, and indeed to underwrite, the basic assumptions made in conventional education: school is a valuable and beneficial institution; children should accept authority; and they should be taught a prescribed list of traditional subjects. There is little in this philosophy of education that can be seen by teachers as either threatening or unrealistic.

Another reason why the education world took notice of the new philosophy of education is that this kind of writing looked academically reputable and rigorous. Unlike Rousseau, Peters wrote in a cultural atmosphere where the highest accolades had long been reserved for scientific forms of study. The prevailing view was that any enquiry which is to establish sound answers must be: (i) detached, impersonal, unemotional; (ii) precise, methodical, orderly; and (iii) small-scale, piecemeal, cautious. These are today the hallmarks of rationality, and they are not to be found in Rousseau, whose style is by these standards dubiously intuitive. The new philosophy of education, by contrast, was produced by professional academics. In their writing, Peters and Dearden proceed cautiously, and generate conclusions which verge on the conventional.

As far as rigour is concerned, there is a serious discrepancy between the nature of their own writing and the role which is advocated for philosophers in the course of this writing. Dearden reminds us that the Plowden Report is a work of recommendation (Peters, 1969, p. 24), though few readers of the report will need to have this pointed out. Philosophers of education are not so keen to advertise the fact that much of their own writing is of the same logical character. What they do say about their own writing tends to suggest something else: it is a second-order activity which characteristically proceeds by way of conceptual analysis. Some of this kind of work has been reviewed in last chapter's discussion of what philosophers have said about the concepts of 'needs' and 'growth': here their writing seems to suggest that the philosophical mind, penetrating and detached, has detected values disguised as facts, and aims statements presented as scientifically based. Saved from this kind of deception, those who read such work may feel justified in deciding henceforth to put their trust only in philosophers.

But even if these philosophers of education were analytical philosophers, they were not *just* analytical philosophers. These writers were advancing an alternative to child-centred education: their preferred approach involves the initiation of children into differentiated forms of knowledge on the grounds that these intellectual disciplines constitute the most valuable of human activities. In this approach the organizing principles of education are to be determined primarily by a traditional conception of the nature of knowledge rather than by the nature of the child. As was shown at the end of Chapter 7, the philosophers' advocacy of this approach is on the *same logical level* as the recommendations of the Plowden Report, and it is no more intellectually compelling.

The writing of Peters, Hirst and Dearden, however, has appeared to carry more authority, because philosophers have presented themselves as conducting a dispassionate clear-sighted enquiry from a viewpoint distanced from (if not elevated above) the partisan wranglings of competing and contentious approaches to education. Here is how Peters explains the standing of his writing: 'I, like Scheffler in America, came from a philosophy department and shared his conviction that analytic philosophy, which was the currently accepted orthodoxy, had much to offer to education. So there was the authority of an established discipline behind the work' (Peters, 1983, p. 36). The use of perceived academic authority to discredit child-centred concepts was intended to help reinstate a more conservative approach to the curriculum. But this counter-revolution was not just about pedagogy. It may be better explained in terms of Peters' distinctive view of man and society.

In the 1960s, with its unsettling rejection of the old ways, some saw the threat of serious disorder, and many looked askance at non-authoritarian classrooms. Deep in Peters' *Ethics and Education*, the classic textbook of the new philosophy of education, we find this revealing passage:

> Progressive schools in which the staff, as a matter of policy, withdraw from their proper function of exercising a just and levelling form of social control, are notorious for peer-group pressure and the proliferation of rules administered with severity by the children themselves. Or something like a state of nature prevails, as depicted with ghoulish exaggeration by William Golding in his *Lord of the Flies*. I once asked a colleague why his parents took him away from one of these schools. He replied that it was such hell when the headmaster was not around because of the bullying that went on.
>
> (Peters, 1966a, p. 194)

The regrettable truth, however, is that bullying was a feature of school life long before schools felt the impact of child-centred educational theory. Peters' evident horror of a state of nature and the pessimistic view of children which this quotation reveals show how far the modern philosopher of education is removed from writers like Rousseau. Orderly life in society is, for Peters, highly precarious; behind his strictures on child-centred education lies an image of 'the awesome spectacle of human beings trying to sustain and cultivate a crust of civilization over the volcanic core of atavistic emotions' (Peters, 1972, p. 87). Ultimately Peters' apparent desire to halt the advance of the child-centred movement may be explicable in terms of a cautious social conservatism. At the end of *Ethics and Education* we are told that we should 'come to realize that the most worthwhile features of political life are immanent in the institutions which we in fact have' (Peters, 1966a, p. 319). One could not ask for a better illustration of the difference in outlook between modern philosophers of education and the eighteenth-century writer who is sometimes seen as having lit the long, slow fuse which led to the French Revolution.

Such promotion of the philosopher's values is directly at odds with Peters' own model of philosophy as dispassionate analysis carried out by a detached spectator; and this raises serious questions about the potency, and legitimacy, of his criticism. The tension between child-centred education and modern philosophy of education has generally been accepted as one where a fashionably developmental ideology is exposed by technical experts as intellectually dubious. It is more correctly seen as a clash between two opposing ideologies. Once this is understood, the authority of the philosophers' critique is dramatically diminished.

Historically, however, there seems to have been an inflated estimate of its cogency: the philosophers' critique has been seen as fatal to the credibility of child-centred education rather than as a challenge to produce a clearer rationale. The practical importance of this perception is related to the child-centred teacher's need for confidence. Where education follows long-established norms, few questions will be asked. Where teachers or policy-makers adopt new ideas, they must be prepared to defend their practice, for this will inevitably be viewed with misgivings. Innovative teaching has to proceed with an eye to self-justification. But it is hard to maintain the necessary morale for this once it is felt that the underlying principles will not stand up to critical scrutiny.

What may have caused such a feeling to spread was perhaps not so much that Peters and Dearden pronounced child-centred educational theory to be intellectually dubious, as that practically every philosopher of education in the country appeared to share this view. Teachers may well have been impressed by the spectacle of near unanimity among those seen as independent-minded thinkers. The rest of this chapter will explore the background to this remarkable accord. The explanation lies in the career of R. S. Peters, in the position he occupied in philosophy of education, and in concurrent developments in teacher training.

At the end of Chapter 4 we noted that college staff were early converts to progressivism, and that in the 1960s these institutions were involved in massive expansion. But the colleges were not just to grow in numbers: they were also to grow in stature. In 1963 the Robbins Report recommended that training colleges should be retitled 'colleges of education', and that they should prepare some of their students for a new B.Ed. degree. This involvement in the planning and teaching of degree courses triggered off what Joan Browne describes as a 'search for academic and theoretical substance' (Browne, 1987, p. 92). For non-university institutions to establish their academic credibility it was not enough that their courses should be of the right kind – they had to be *seen* to be of the right kind. This was the spring to a policy of conspicuous academicism. The part of the college curriculum which was identified as having the necessary potential was educational studies. B.Ed. students would have to learn to study education with the kind of rigour that would confer academic status on this activity. And they would have to be taught by lecturers with appropriately academic backgrounds.

In 1964 the Department of Education and Science (DES) suggested that a conference be held to discuss the nature of educational studies. One of the speakers was R. S. Peters, by then professor of philosophy of education at the London University Institute of Education. In a seminal paper he identified what he called 'the foundation disciplines of philosophy, psychology, and sociology', all subjects whose natural habitat was clearly the university (Peters, 1964). At a later stage, history was added to this influential list.

Why was the educational world so willing to let Peters define the correct approach to educational studies? The answer lies in a combination of two factors: he had an impressive academic record in a traditional university discipline; and he seemed to be developing the application of rigorous thought to education in a new way that promised to produce important insights. It would be surprising if this prospect had not generated excitement.

Teachers in the Institute of Education have often exercised extraordinary influence. Much as Susan Isaacs revitalized the study of child development in this country when she went to London from her experience at the Malting House School, so Peters brought a new standing to the philosophy of education by bringing with him credentials from a different, but related field. Peters was a reader in philosophy at Birkbeck College and had published in the history of philosophy, social and political philosophy, and philosophical psychology. He had more than won his spurs in a 'hard' discipline and his move to the Institute was instrumental in helping philosophy of education to lose some of its 'marshmallow' image. Many lecturers who had an interest in this area of education were at that time uncertain about the kind of contribution they could or should make. Here at last was a philosopher who was talking and writing about education in a way that commanded general respect. In philosophy of education Peters rapidly took up a position of absolute dominance: as one of his colleagues puts it, Peters 'not only redefined British philosophy of education but set its programme for some twenty years' (Hirst, 1986, p. 8). How was this brought about?

In 1966, as well as publishing *Ethics and Education*, Peters founded the Philosophy of Education Society of which he became chairman. The society published the proceedings of its annual conference, and this volume in time was superseded by a twice-yearly publication, *The Journal of Philosophy of Education*: Peters was the editor. Where a discipline identifies with a single journal, the contents of the journal can readily be seen as defining the field. The editors are therefore in a highly influential position. By including some articles, and excluding others, they can lay down what constitutes good philosophy of education (or good curriculum theory or good sociology of knowledge) and what does not.

Peters also edited *The Concept of Education* (1967), a collection of papers written by a number of philosophers both unknown and well established. The latter group included Max Black, John Passmore and Gilbert Ryle. The editor's strategy in assembling the material was remarkably directive, and is best explained in Peters' own words:

> It was felt that merely providing a general title such as 'The Concept of Education' was insufficient to provide . . . a unifying theme . . . . The editor therefore wrote the first article attempting to map the main contours of the concept, circulated it, and invited lecturers and contributors to sketch in one of the important areas in more detail.
> (Peters, 1967, p. vii)

This passage is revealing in two ways. First, it assumes a consensus view of what is involved in education – hence the title '*The* Concept of Education'. The suggestion is that this is a matter that can be quietly sorted out once our thinking on education is shorn of emotionalism and partisanship and taken over by reasonable people trained in rigorous thinking. The book is presented as a work of logical geography, and one would not expect cartographers – even philosophical cartographers – to engage in ideological struggle.

Second, Peters' conception of his editorial role suggests an unusual relationship between the contributors and the editor. One possibility is that Peters' account of how he approached his collaborators is inaccurate. If it *is* accurate, it is an interesting comment on Peters' standing at this time that so many people were prepared to be seen as filling in the details of the editor's own position. Whatever the truth about the mechanics of its compilation, the volume brought together a formidable list of writers whose essays had a fair degree of mutual coherence both in tone and content. Much the same could be said of another collection in which the editor gratefully records: 'R. S. Peters was particularly helpful in his suggestions regarding the scope of the book, and the authors who might contribute to it' (Archambault, 1965, p. ix). A further opportunity for Peters to define the territory arose with the publication of J. W. Tibble's book *The Study of Education* (1966). This blueprint for a reformulated programme of educational studies publicly portrayed the subject as an amalgam of foundation disciplines, this time giving history of education parity with the other three. Each educational discipline was outlined in a separate chapter written by a leading practitioner in the field. At that time philosophy of education had one, and only one, 'leading practitioner' – R. S. Peters. Tibble also became general editor of an influential series of books, Routledge & Kegan Paul's 'Students' Library of Education', which was designed on the basis of these disciplinary divisions. The editor for books on philosophy of education in this series was again Peters.

For the developing colleges of education, the attraction of viewing educational studies as consisting of subjects rooted in established disciplines like philosophy had a more mundane dimension than considerations of academic status. Organizationally this formula suggested something neat and manageable: a framework of semi-independent specialist courses. Browne describes a consequence of this new conception: 'there was a move away from the "all purpose" education tutor towards the specialist in one of the educational disciplines, that is psychology, sociology, philosophy, and history as applied to education, often a well qualified young academic appointed to meet the needs of the expanding colleges' (Browne, 1987, p. 920). This accords with Peters' demand made at the 1964 conference that 'there should be at least one specialist in philosophy of education on every staff. And by that I mean someone with a training in philosophy, not in the history of ideas' (Peters, 1964, pp. 147–8). Having told colleges what was required, Peters went on to identify an obvious problem and then to solve it: 'The difficulty . . . is to get staff who are both experienced teachers and also trained in one or more of the foundation disciplines . . . . We are only making a beginning with training such specialists at London with our new MA' (Peters, 1964, pp. 147–9).

No doubt the scorn poured on the way colleges had previously handled philosophy (see Chapter 6) helped to persuade these institutions of the need to appoint a new breed of philosophy lecturer. For the expanding colleges, there was one, and only one, obvious unit which could produce potential lecturers who were familiar with the new approach to philosophy of education. Peters confirms that 'a large percentage' of British philosophers of education graduated from the London Institute's philosophy of education department (Peters, 1983, p. 36).

What did Peters' students learn and how did they learn it? Clearly

Peters' course would be informed by what he says in general terms about the importance of teaching. One of the criticisms levelled by the new philosophers at the Plowden Report was that while it had a lot to say about how children learn, it did not sufficiently stress the need for teaching: teachers, they argued, should teach. Peters' conception of education as initiation likewise commits him to the view that learning necessarily involves teachers: 'The procedures of a discipline can only be mastered by an exploration of its established content under the guidance of one who has already been initiated' (Peters, 1966a, p. 54). He stresses this as a necessary corrective to what he sees as the fashionable emphasis on 'individual exploration and experimentation'.

For a 1960s course on philosophy of education, 'exploration of established content' inevitably meant the study of *Ethics and Education* and similar material rather than an 'antiquated diet' of Rousseau and Dewey. And in this context the necessary 'guidance of one who has already been initiated' can only refer to the teaching of Peters and his colleagues. (It is significant that Peters cites as one of the defects of philosophy of education prior to the 1960s the fact that it was 'variously interpreted', though it is hard to see why this should be construed as a demerit.) Finally we should note that on this model of learning and teaching, the teacher becomes dispensable after the initiation process. The difference between the teacher and the learner becomes only one of degree once the learner 'has built into his mind both the concepts and mode of exploration involved' (Peters, 1966a, p. 53).

So students who trained in London and went on to teach philosophy of education elsewhere would probably have been expected to internalize Peters' conception of the subject and how to do it. But as we have seen, what was presented as analytical technique involved commitment to a substantive view of education. As Peters himself tellingly observes, 'initiation' suggests 'an avenue of access to a body of belief'. So when a college of education was recruiting someone with the most reputable specialist qualification in the subject to teach philosophy of education to its B.Ed. students, it was (possibly unwittingly) acquiring a lecturer (i) whose views on the curriculum were opposed to progressive primary practice, (ii) who shared Peters' assessment of the Plowden model of the teacher, that 'there is so much wrong with this image that one scarcely knows where to begin criticising it' (Peters, 1969, p. 16), and (iii) who felt that the erroneous nature of child-centred education could be demonstrated by non-partisan analysis. This would seem the inevitable result of the initiation process.

Was a training course of the kind offered by Peters really necessary? 'Initiation' suggests mystery, where secrets can only be revealed by a master. But it may be argued that there is little mystery involved in doing philosophy. While some philosophical books are plain hard going, there is no secret key to unravelling what is said. Other philosophical writing is quite accessible and such books are doubtless read by many outwith the ranks of professional philosophers. Among these readers one might reasonably expect to find schoolteachers, highly educated people some of whom will have studied some philosophy at university. These people are ideally placed to think and write philosophically about education. But once the idea of a qualification in philosophy of education becomes accepted, those without it are in danger of being seen as, and of seeing themselves as, 'unqualified'. So the subject may well have been deprived of a whole range of potential contributors because of the importance attached to a course of training in a particular institution.

Instead of there being diverse contributions, one institution was able to define the subject by a steady flow of books, all of which struck a remarkably similar tone. The sameness of so much writing in philosophy of education is far from satisfactory. 'Aridity' and 'destructiveness' may not be unusual charges for philosophers to face, but 'uniformity' and 'derivativeness' are strange characteristics to find in a discipline where fundamental questioning is crucial. Despite Ayer's disapproval of philo-sophical 'parties', philosophers *ought* to be perpetually challenging each other. Such challenges were not a prominent feature of philosophy of education in the 1960s and 1970s.

An indication of what was studied in college by trainee teachers on philosophy of education courses is available from a 1982 *Times Educa-tional Supplement* survey of course textbooks (Homan, 1982). Of the twenty texts most frequently prescribed in pre-service training, three were philosophy books: *Problems in Primary Education*, by R. F. Dearden (1976); *Knowledge and the Curriculum*, by P. H. Hirst (1974); and *The Logic of Education*, by P. H. Hirst and R. S. Peters (1970). The survey explained that the only reason Peters did not feature more prominently was that 'votes' for him were distributed over a number of titles. The survey also draws attention to the absence of Plato and Rousseau 'neither of whom has published anything recently'.

So colleges of education were often effectively transmitting two contra-dictory messages. Since the war they had been committed to the principles of Froebel and Hadow; and their conviction that this was the right approach was undoubtedly strengthened by the publication of the Plowden Report and the Primary Memorandum. Yet the view implicit (and sometimes explicit) in the books used on philosophy of education courses was that child-centred education was incoherent, confused, and intellectually unrespectable.

Those immersed in the traditions of child-centred thinking are some-times lacking in intellectual bite: in this situation, they may not have had the critical tools, or the academic clout, for answering back. But there was a further difficulty. The champions of child-centred education were often in colleges of education. The new standing of the colleges was seen as depending on their academic credibility. This in turn rested on giving a central place to educational studies, in which philosophy of education was seen as playing an impressively rigorous part. For these child-centred educationists to dismiss the philosophers' contribution would have been to risk sawing off the branch of the tree of knowledge on which they were perched.

Despite this petrified silence from the world of teacher training, this book has argued that the logic of the philosophers' criticisms was not such as to destroy the theoretical foundations of child-centred education. Some of the criticisms seem misplaced, at least as far as contemporary statements of progressivism are concerned. Some of the analysis could (and should) be taken on board by child-centred theorists as a contribution to the clarification of the progressive position. In general terms, the authority that was claimed for the philosophers' critique was lacking because it was not conducted from the promised position of detachment. The near unanimity with which professional philosophers of education adopted Peters' anti-progressive stance owed little to the merits of the case and much to the way these philosophers became 'qualified'.

9

THE BLACK PAPER YEARS

Despite the debatable value of its deliberations, philosophy of education effectively undermined confidence in the intellectual credibility of child-centred education and thus made it more vulnerable to other pressures. These pressures will now be examined. The movement against child-centred education began as a series of responses to Plowden. In this chapter we move from the philosophical response, to the populist and the political.

As we have seen, the Plowden Committee did not have to wait long before seeing its thinking subjected to some powerful challenges: 1969 saw the appearance of *Perspectives on Plowden* where R. S. Peters in fact produced two rather different perspectives (on the same page):

- the general view of education taken in the Report . . . is far from appropriate to the practical needs of our time.
- we certainly believe that by and large they [the Reports recommendations] would, if carried out, lead to a marked improvement in primary school education.

(Peters, 1969, p. ix)

The main feature which these observations have in common is that both reflect the kind of broad judgement which Peters had earlier declared to be beyond the scope of philosophy.

The same year also saw the publication of the first two Black Papers – collections of vigorously critical articles written from various positions, but predominantly from the political right. Five such collections were published, the first three being edited by Brian Cox and A. E. Dyson, the last two by Cox and Rhodes Boyson. Boyson rose to prominence as a vociferous headmaster, became influential in the Conservative Party, and finished up as an MP and, from 1979 to 1983, an education minister. Much later, Cox was appointed by the government to chair a committee on the teaching of English.

The first two editors were teachers in the university sector, and, not surprisingly, the impetus for producing the first Black Paper had less to do with schools than with the editors' own professional sphere: it arose from student protests which reached their confrontational peak in May 1968 in the Sorbonne and at Nanterre, and which generated some modest disturbances in Britain. Many university teachers felt unhappy at the prospect of a growth in student power: unrest was readily seen as rebellion and anarchy. The first Black Paper was largely concerned with such developments in higher education: schooling was invoked primarily to serve as an explanation for the breakdown in order.

The basic argument was that because schools (particularly primary schools) were no longer teaching children to respect authority, these young people subsequently lacked a disciplined approach to their university studies. This argument may be facile, since the emergence of new ideas about discipline and authority in both primary education and higher education clearly has to be understood within a much broader context of the development of new attitudes in society as a whole. But criticisms of the argument on grounds of chronology have scarcely been fair. Alexander (1992) (amongst others) has counter-argued that Plowden children must have progressed very rapidly to universities since the report was published only one year before the student protests. In reality, however, as has been pointed out already in this book, progressive influences were at work much earlier in many primary schools, including those visited by the Plowden Committee itself. The argument from Cox and Dyson quite reasonably points to the germinal contribution of (amongst others) Froebel:

> Influenced by a variety of psychologists from Freud to Piaget, as well as by educational pioneers from Froebel onwards, these schools have increasingly swung away from the notion (which characterises secondary education) that education exists to fit certain sorts of people for certain sorts of jobs, qualifications and economic roles, to the idea that people should develop in their own way at their own pace. . . .
> Competition has given way to self-expression. And now this has worked its way up to the student generation. They don't want to be chivvied through exams on to a career ladder: they want to be (what they conceive to be) themselves: and if the system stands in the way of this, marching about Vietnam in some indefinable way enables them to make a protest against the system and in favour of something better.
>
> (Cox and Dyson, 1969a, p. 6)

In the second Black Paper, articles on higher education were confined to the last part of the text. The writing was more thoughtful and better documented. The highlight was perhaps an article on discovery methods by G. H. Bantock in which he argues that such a method may foster what he calls a magpie curriculum (Bantock, 1969). The topic is tackled through a critique of Rousseau in the course of which Bantock points out that, although Rousseau dichotomizes book learning and discovery learning, you can discover a great deal from books. The second Black Paper also cited R. S. Peters as endorsing the view that the Plowden picture of the teacher is naive. Together, the first two Black Papers sold 80,000 copies.

Were they read sympathetically? One of the editors has recently argued that, although (perhaps because) the Black Papers disputed most of the prevailing conventional wisdom, they were in accord with the views of many parents and teachers. These views had not previously found expression because they were so unfashionable. The novelty and popularity of the Black Papers lay in their successful breaking of a taboo on criticizing a set of policies to which the educational and political establishments were then firmly committed (Cox, 1992, p. 4). When the first volume came out, much of it appeared 'to those of us brought up in the free progressive atmosphere of English education' (said the Secretary of State) 'to be archaic rubbish'. The prime minister, Harold Wilson, denounced it in Parliament, where he took care to suggest that his own educational policies were very much in line with those of some Conservative predecessors: 'I totally reject . . . the attitudes and arguments used in this so-called "black" paper about the whole liberal progress in education carried forward for over twenty years now' (quoted in Cox, 1992, p. 175).

At the time, leading educational opinion in Edward Heath's Conservative Party would undoubtedly have endorsed this rejection. It is a significant measure of the dramatic change in Conservative educational thinking that by 1977 the utterances of the fifth Black Paper had come to reflect the dominant view within the Conservative Party. The editors' introduction urged that

> the national monitoring of basic standards by examinations for all children at the ages of 7, 11 and 14 or 15 should be introduced. The school results of these tests should be available to parents, school governors and the local community. Children's names should not be published, but parents have a right to know the comparative achievements of schools.
>
> (Cox and Boyson, 1977, p. 8)

This was the blend of market philosophy and strong central government which commended itself to the new party leader, Margaret Thatcher, and which eventually led to the imposition of a national curriculum. In Cox's view the conversion of the school system into an education market appealed to parents because it offered to liberate them from the dictates of bureaucrats and educationists, whose theories were seen as having led to lower standards of attainment in basic skills.

The Black Papers can thus be used as a barometer for indicating the transformation in climate from the progressivism of the Plowden era. When the first two Black Papers appeared in 1969, their ideas appeared too deviant to be taken seriously: their authors were seen as constituting the irresponsible lunatic fringe of their time. Ten years later, the political party which came round to wholehearted adoption of Black Paper thinking captured the popular vote and thus came to power.

All three Black Paper editors were themselves working-class boys who had made good through traditional schooling; they seem to have resented the suggestion that this was not the kind of educational experience that children should now be given, seeing some new policies as a novel form of educational deprivation. Cox makes a point of arguing that some of the critics of the Black Papers came to prominence without having had quite the same struggle: Anthony Crosland, Shirley Williams and Professor Brian Simon were from distinctly privileged backgrounds, although the curriculum to which they were exposed was no doubt broadly similar to Cox's own.

Another success story with a lowly social starting point was Labour's fourth, and most conservative, prime minister, James Callaghan. Callaghan's principal policy adviser has been cited as maintaining that the prime minister 'believed passionately . . . in the need for rigorous educational standards to enable working class youngsters to rise above their circumstances' (Chitty, 1989, p. 68). Just as Wilson referred back to earlier Conservative administrations to indicate cross-party consensus, Callaghans famous 1976 speech at Ruskin College was destined to be invoked by subsequent Conservative governments to suggest that their policies represented common sense rather than a partisan party line. Even though it contained a tart remark about 'Black Paper prejudice', the tone of the Ruskin speech (Callaghan, 1976) was such that it could even be welcomed by Rhodes Boyson himself (Chitty, 1989, p. 97).

Callaghan said three things which are relevant to the concerns of this chapter. First, he recognized, without explicitly endorsing, 'the unease felt by parents and teachers about the new informal methods of teaching'. Secondly, he gave voice to the idea of a 'core curriculum of basic knowledge'. Most fundamental, however, was his insistence that the views of politicians, parents and others should be made to count, and that educational debate could not properly be left exclusively to professional teachers. In presenting dissent from this view as advice to 'keep off the grass', Callaghan was alluding to an earlier political speech made by an education minister who, frustrated in his attempts to influence what was taught in schools and training colleges, coined the phrase 'the secret garden of the curriculum.' 'Of course', said Sir David Eccles in 1960, 'Parliament would never attempt to dictate the curriculum' (Chitty, 1989, p. 132). Indeed, in law, Parliament was in no position to do that, though of course the law could always be changed. In 1985 a DES White Paper was still able to reaffirm the traditional position: 'The government does not propose to introduce legislation affecting the powers of the Secretary of State in relation to the curriculum' (DES, 1985, p. 12). In the years that followed, however, traditional positions counted for nothing.

The unease about new informal methods to which Callaghan alluded had been given two significant boosts in the period preceding Ruskin. The first came with the virtual collapse of one London primary school where the majority of teachers were dedicated to their own form of 'progressivism'. The second event was the publication of a piece of educational research apparently showing that informal methods were less effective than traditional methods. It might, of course, be argued that it was not these developments *per se* which fed public unease, but the publicity given to them. Undoubtedly the media to some extent *created* unease as well as reporting and reflecting it. But public disquiet clearly predated the publicity; indeed, had there been no such concern in the first instance, the media would probably have paid little attention to these events.

The stated aims of William Tyndale School cited Plowden approvingly and spoke of the importance of blurring subject divisions. The teacher in charge of the youngest children seems to have been a classic Plowden progressive, abolishing rote learning and introducing group teaching. But the dominant faction among teachers of older children in the school was much more radical: indeed, the head of infants was criticized by her colleagues for adopting such a moderate form of progressivism (Gretton and Jackson, 1976). The enquiry which was ultimately launched in 1975 into the school's teaching described the philosophy of the leading radical: 'For him the essence of teaching is to encourage his pupils, however young, to take their own decisions about learning' (Auld, 1976, p. 42). This approach to education clearly lies outside the child-centred tradition developed through Pestalozzi and Froebel, and is allied more closely to the libertarian ideas famously practised in A. S. Neill's Summerhill School. However, what may well attract the support of a small number of parents who are choosing a school in the private sector is unlikely to be acceptable in a local primary school. According to the report of the enquiry, 'Mr Haddow and Mr Ellis (the headteacher) expressed their attitudes in such a way as to suggest that they had lost all sense of balance in the changes that they wished to make' (Auld, 1976, p. 74). Added to the radical nature of the approach was a disinclination to implement the philosophy in a manner that was organized and disciplined. Further, the school served the kind of area which would be likely to generate difficulties for even the most resourceful of teachers, promoted or unpromoted. This combination of factors led to a highly disorderly school and a deterioration of relationships between staff and parents, culminating in official intervention.

The fact that practice in William Tyndale was an extreme, and incompetently handled, version of progressivism did not deter the press from exploiting the scandal to feed the anxieties of all parents of primary-age children. In London, the *Evening News* professed to think that extreme methods were being practised everywhere: 'People all over London have been concerned at the revolutionary teaching methods being introduced in the city's schools' (quoted in Ellis *et al.*, 1976, p. 154). The *Daily Express* observed: 'The exposure of teaching methods and appalling results at William Tyndale School, London, has alerted parents everywhere to the need to find out what is going on in the classroom' (Ellis *et al.*, 1976, p. 157). In the *Daily Telegraph* Rhodes Boyson portrayed teaching at the William Tyndale School as part of a sinister socialist strategy in a spectacular sentence which leaves the reader wondering who is the extremist: 'It is a favourite trick of the extreme left to destroy all values and all morality and to create what Trotsky called "human dust"' (Ellis *et al.*, 1976, p. 157).

The dangers of generalizing from particular cases are familiar enough to anyone who thinks seriously about education. In a vast system of state schooling, there is always the potential for institutional disaster. It may be inevitable that these schools are used as whipping boys for national and social and even personal problems. The danger for 'progressive' teachers is that they are seen by the public as claiming to know better than the layperson, who was generally educated along quite different lines. Where there is latent resentment, any shortcomings make progressive education highly vulnerable to criticism. Provoking people to indulge in the pleasures of censoriousness and outrage, like the titillation of sexual desire, has always been a profitable business for the media.

Nor were the Black Papers above giving a platform to this kind of generalization from the particular. The 1977 collection featured an article by Dolly Walker, William Tyndale's dissenting member of staff, who described the school's philosophy as 'having vague connotations with Rousseau's concept of the child being allowed to develop "naturally" at his own pace without undue influence' (Walker, 1977, p. 38) Walker, depending on one's point of view, had engaged in a heroic struggle with this philosophy by alerting parents and others to what was happening, or had engaged in professional behaviour described by the enquiry as 'disgraceful'. Whichever is the fairer account, the theme she developed was becoming familiar: 'the William Tyndale confrontation . . . has at last disclosed the depths to which education has sunk. . . the debasement of education which it exemplifies is a reflection of a very widespread *malaise* within education in this country today' (Walker, 1977, p. 38).

By this time, however, further ammunition for the critics had appeared from a very different quarter with the publication of Neville Bennett's *Teaching Styles and Pupil Progress* in 1976. This book reported an empirical study of how far primary pupils progressed over the period of a year in different classes where the teachers style was classified as either 'formal', 'informal' or 'mixed'. Bennett found that pupils in formal classrooms made progress in reading, maths, and the understanding of English which was significantly superior to the progress made by those taught informally. There was declared to be an 'unequivocal' association between formal teaching methods and 'progress in the basic skills' (Bennett, 1976a). A television programme on Bennett's research was produced and broadcast to coincide with the publication of the book.

The message seemed clear, and the findings were just what the media required. The immediate publicity was on a scale seldom dreamed of by an educational researcher.

The day the book appeared, 26 April 1976, press coverage was extensive. The *Daily Express* quoted Brian Cox: 'This vindicates everything we have been saying in the last seven years. Thousands of teachers have been trained since the Plowden Report was published in 1967. We now know they have been given the wrong ideas.' *The Times* reported Cox as saying that a counter-revolution was now required.

A *Daily Telegraph* leader on 'these lunatic methods' began by suggesting that Bennett's findings were hardly surprising, at least to sensible people: 'It has often been remarked that expert, factual reports into commonplace aspects of contemporary life tend to confirm, somewhat belatedly, what ordinary people have always known to be true.' The leader concludes by offering a speculative suggestion for a future research programme:

> we are told [that] progressive teachers do not aim at academic results so much as at 'social and moral growth', much less measurable commodities. One cannot help suspecting, however, that a study of the relationship between vandalism and teacher-bashing and informal methods might lead many parents to opt for the 3Rs.
> (Daily Telegraph, 1976, p. 3)

Despite the confidence he displayed in his own findings, Bennett did not endorse reactions of the kind offered to the public by the media, though he must have known that these conclusions would in fact be drawn. Writing in the *Guardian*, he observed, a little optimistically, 'It is hoped that the findings will not be used as a slogan for a "back to formal teaching" movement.' (Bennett, 1976b) This judgement may reflect a finding reported in his book that one of the classes which was taught informally had particularly high gains in every achievement area. It may also reflect an awareness of other research studies which had tended to generate rather inconclusive results (Rogers and Barron, 1976).

The methodology of Bennett's study was subjected to considerable scrutiny and criticism ('not surprisingly', Brian Cox later observed (Cox, 1992, p. 218)). Questions were asked about whether Bennett's groups of teachers were equally experienced and whether the classes of pupils were matched for comparable social class composition. On more technical points the critique grew to the point where a research team, of which Bennett was a member, decided to reanalyse the data. This resulted, in the team's own words, in 'greatly reduced significance of any differences'. Progress in English was greater in formal classes; progress in reading was greater in informal classes; and 'in mathematics the formal and informal styles are close' (Aitkin, Bennett and Hesketh, 1981). This time the results were published in an academic journal: there was no television programme broadcasting the news to the nation.

10

THE CURRICULUM
AND THE PROFESSION

It is impossible to gauge the relative importance of a single book like *Teaching Styles and Pupil Progress*, a series of publications like the Black Papers, and the reporting of the failings of an individual school. However, it is beyond dispute that the combined impact of all of these was massive. Cox's own view of the effectiveness of the Black Papers may not be too unrealistic:

> The Black Papers liberated a repressed ideology which eventually was to play a part in making Mrs Thatcher Prime Minister in 1979. Their success in transforming the educational scene was a triumph for the ordinary, the obvious, the instinctive and the natural over the theorists and utopians of the 1960s.
>
> (Cox, 1992, p. 4)

The early Black Papers set the scene by linking concern over educational standards with fears about social disintegration. William Tyndale seemed to provide a graphic illustration of both. Bennett confirmed many people's suspicions of progressive teaching. Teachers and educational theorists alike came to be seen as culpable, not just for low scholastic attainment, but for a host of other social ills. From Ruskin onwards there were increasingly strong hints of government support for this view.

This climate provided the springboard for major change – not least in the view taken of the freedom enjoyed by schools and local education authorities to determine the nature of the education provided for primary-age pupils. Once proudly exhibited as a characteristically English freedom which gave maximum scope to professional initiatives, both individual and co-operative, this came to be seen as a crucial weakness in a failing system. In its place came a national curriculum, put into effect by force of law, consisting of ten 'core' and 'foundation' subjects plus religious education. This was to be bolstered by an intensive programme of attainment tests with schools' performances made public – a system of 'accountability' designed to put pressure on schools and teachers.

It had proved significantly easy for the government to seize the high ground. Since teachers and education authorities seemed unable to put their own house in order, the government would have to do it for them: indeed this was a duty it owed to the people of the country. And decisive action was made all the more attractive by the realization that there was electoral advantage to be gained: taking a big stick to teachers proved almost as popular as taking a hard line on law and order.

The idea of tests for primary children at different stages is scarcely novel, as has been pointed out with relish by those unsympathetic to the idea. In 1862 the Revised Code defined six standards of attainment in reading, writing and arithmetic. For reading, Standard I required 'narrative in monosyllables'; and Standard VI required the pupil to be able to read a paragraph from a newspaper. Testing was carried out by a visiting inspector: the school's income, and therefore the teacher's, depended on the results.

The reintroduction of this last feature has not, at the time of writing, been seriously advocated, although in the present climate nothing can be confidently ruled out. One way of reinforcing this sense of the difficulty of forecasting policy development is to look back at an article published in 1980 by Ted Wragg with the title 'State approved knowledge? Ten steps down the slippery slope'. Here Wragg is fantasizing about the possibility of state control being gradually increased up to a 'highly undesirable' level. At the time this was commonly read as a doomsday scenario, as scaremongering – perhaps even partly as a joke. Since then England has moved from the first step, 'centrally prescribed broad aims' through 'centrally prescribed objectives' to Step 9, 'publication of results by school'. Wragg comments: 'This could be a most powerful form of central control . . . . Inevitably most teachers' time and energy would be spent on those aspects of the curriculum which were to be systematically tested and publicly rank-ordered' (Wragg, 1980, p. 18). Only Step 10 of the fantasy has not been formally realized: 'dismissal of teachers who fail to deliver'.

Recent developments in Scotland have shown interesting differences. While Scottish outlines for a curriculum for ages five to fourteen have again been produced centrally, these are less detailed and less restrictive in their specifications; they are produced by committees of professionals; and officially they have only the status of 'guidance'. The primary curriculum is thought of in terms of five areas with history and geography being deprived of clear separate identities. The proposal to produce curriculum guidelines originally met with resistance from teachers, but perhaps because of the powerful role allotted to the profession (or at least to some of its well-placed members) became clear, opposition faded. The 'guidelines' will certainly be implemented, perhaps with a little pressure from the Inspectorate, but without any recourse to law. The Scottish Office Education Department (1993) circular which accompanies the Guidelines on Environmental Studies simply observes: 'The Secretary of State commends the Guidelines and invites Education Authorities and schools to incorporate them as soon as possible in the teaching of Environmental Studies.'

By contrast, the original proposals for testing in Scotland proved anathema to teachers, to education authorities and to parents, many of whom decided to keep their children away from school when testing was in progress. In the face of this combination of forces, the government had no choice but to give way on all the more contentious points. Tests are now to be used when teachers see fit in order to check their own judgements about a child's progress through the curriculum. Schools can choose the test units they wish to use with their pupils from a catalogue produced by the Scottish Examination Board.

There are social and historical factors which account for the differences in the way policy has been developed in Scotland. North of the border there is a long and strong tradition of genuinely 'public' schooling, typified by the large high school in each burgh which also served (and still serves) the rural hinterland. Self-made men and women from impoverished backgrounds achieved success *through* education, not, as often happened in England, despite their lack of it. Success has tended to be thought of in terms of entry to the professions, including teaching. The Presbyterian church, which over centuries maintained a powerful influence over the school system, demanded a literate Bible-reading population and a highly educated ministry. And a proud working class with a genuinely socialist tradition has ensured that the Conservative power-base in Scotland tends to be relatively frail. The Thatcherite minister who promoted the five-to-fourteen curriculum and the testing programme was transferred to a London ministry for fear his ideas would damage the Conservative cause among the natives. It is not surprising that in such a culture primary teachers seemed to develop a no-nonsense version of child-centred education that was clearly compatible with sound learning. There were no spectacular excesses to upset the public and discredit the underlying philosophy. Consequently there was no obvious reason for government intervention: parents of primary-school children seemed reasonably satisfied with their schools.

Despite all this, the differences between the new curriculum policies north and south of the border remain relative, and should not be overemphasized. Both reflect the belief that a set of bureaucratic prescriptions is not just appropriate, but desirable. Once formulated and in place, these prescriptions, in both England and Scotland, seem to be effectively removed from further debate. Yet it is the developments in England which give greater cause for concern. The design of the curriculum in terms of a list of subjects constitutes a particularly sharp rebuff to progressive teachers in primary education who see themselves as having a more sophisticated and less simplistic conception of knowledge and curriculum. A more fundamental rebuff, however, is the removal from such teachers, by process of law, of the powers of curriculum determination. Progressive teachers see themselves as enlightened and informed practitioners whose professional expertise is underwritten by an advanced understanding of the educational process and of children's cognitive and social development. The assumption here is that this professional knowledge equips teachers to make sound judgements about what curricular fare is appropriate: conversely, it precludes others, who are not informed in these ways, from telling teachers what to teach. More specifically, however, where a child-centred view is taken of education, a crucial factor in the making of sensible decisions about the curriculum is held to be an understanding of individual children in particular social circumstances. The logical conclusion of such an argument is that the person best placed to determine the curriculum is the classroom teacher.

This view is not accepted, and possibly not understood, by politicians, who see this kind of argument as a case of special pleading for teacher power, an excuse to keep the gate of the secret garden bolted. Governments are predisposed to think not in terms of individual children in particular social settings, but of 'the nations children' or 'the next generation': indeed, this is what makes intelligible the concept of a 'national curriculum'. Where curriculum is thought of as differentiated, or even individualized, teachers may reasonably be seen as equipped to make professional judgements on what they should teach: by contrast, government thinking about a future generation inevitably involves broad value judgements of a kind which go beyond the bounds of what can be reserved for professional expertise. The appropriate sphere for this expertise is consequently redefined, in the minds of politicians, in terms of teaching skills.

There has thus been a tendency in official circles to make an emphatic distinction between curriculum content and how this is taught (or 'delivered'). Indeed the government's policy of encouraging parents to choose between schools depends on this distinction: with the imposition of the National Curriculum, schools can no longer vary in curricular terms, so there is nothing here to choose between; but schools may vary in terms of methods, the effectiveness of which will supposedly be revealed by the publication of test scores.

While the first of these two supposedly distinct dimensions of education is now centrally defined with the authority of Parliament, the second has been officially declared to be the preserve of teachers. Thus Kenneth Clarke, for example: 'Questions about how to teach are not for Government to determine' (quoted in Alexander *et al.*, 1992, p. 5). On the face of it, allowing teachers discretionary powers over teaching methods fails to reflect the nature of the parental 'unease' which was originally used to legitimate government involvement. As Callaghan noted, this unease was directed at the 'new informal methods': there was no evident disquiet among parents or in the press about children's lack of scientific knowledge. While, however, the government eventually acted to ensure that science occupied a prominent place in the primary curriculum, it seemed to see the prescribing of teaching methods as beyond its competence.

In the event, however, the governments declaration of self-restraint on this issue proved to be rhetorical and strategic only. Perhaps they thought that legislation could not readily enforce favoured methods of teaching. Perhaps they feared giving further offence to teachers' professional pride. Most likely, it may have been thought more effective as well as more prudent to engage non-politicians to deliver the required message to the teaching profession.

Child-centred teaching finally fell from official grace in 1992. Just as approval had been indicated through the Plowden Report twenty-five years earlier, ignominy and banishment were signalled by another report produced by three educationists who had been hand-picked by the DES. One was a senior member of the inspectorate; one headed the National Curriculum Council; and the third, Professor Robin Alexander, had already published his observations on primary education in Leeds. Not surprisingly, Alexander *et al.* stated in non-political terms what the government wanted to hear. Their 'discussion paper' dismissed discovery learning, and criticized topic-based enquiry for promoting underachievement. It recommended more subject-based lessons in terms which would not be unacceptable to the philosopher-critics of child-centred education: 'Over the last few decades the progress of primary pupils had been hampered by the influence of highly questionable dogmas which have led to excessively complex practices and devalued the place of subjects in the curriculum' (Alexander *et al.*, 1992, p. 1). It also advised a move towards subject specialization among primary teachers. Finally, the paper recommended more whole-class teaching, the benefits of which were said to be the provision of order, control, purpose and concentration. The Plowden Report had taken three years to complete: its dismissal was written in seven weeks.

Given that colleges of education have, in the past, harboured many enthusiasts for child-centred education, it is significant that Alexander *et al.* make a particular point of redefining teacher education in narrowly functional terms: 'The current priorities for initial training and induction should be the acquisition and strengthening of subject expertise and systematic training in a broad range of classroom organisational strategies and teaching techniques' (*ibid.*, p. 3). The government has itself expressed the wish that as much teacher training as possible should be conducted in schools on an apprenticeship basis. On this view, teaching should be seen as a practical accomplishment which involves acquiring a battery of techniques to be deployed in the delivery of a pre-specified curriculum. ('Delivery' here itself suggests whole-class didacticism, as in the delivery of a speech.) Teaching is not to be seen as an activity informed by educational theory, especially not by *progressive* educational theory.

Following government example, Alexander *et al.* have no qualms about questioning the intelligence of professional teachers: 'If "Plowdenism" has become an ideology to which thousands of teachers have unthinkingly subscribed, then it is necessary to ask why the teachers concerned have stopped thinking for themselves and have apparently become so amenable to indoctrination' (*ibid.*, p. 10). The simplest explanation for so many highly educated people adhering to a cluster of ideas may well be that this 'ideology' (*sic*) contains important truths and valuable insights which are now in danger of being lost. For those in positions of power who fail to grasp these, however, it seems desirable to remove the next generation of teachers from the source of influence. This is undoubtedly what underlies the Secretary of State's view that 'Student teachers need more time in classrooms guided by serving teachers and less time in the teacher training college' (quoted in Lunt, McKenzie and Powell, 1993, p. 143).

If true, the claim that trained teachers are amenable to indoctrination, would clearly be grounds for concern. But the recasting of teacher education in terms of imparting classroom competences manifestly fails to constitute a satisfactory response. A rational response to 'unthinking-ness' in teachers, if this problem does exist, would be to ensure that their courses provide ample scope for the rigorous and critical assessment of alternative conceptions of education and a range of approaches to teaching. There has to be more (perhaps better) educational theory; certainly not less.

The way in which the teaching of educational theory could improve on some earlier practice is not hard to pinpoint. In many colleges in the 1960s and 1970s, adherents of Plowdenism may have argued for Plowden, while followers of R. S. Peters were pressing the claims of the approach which Peters endorsed. Instead of having both schools of thought being presented in different classrooms in one college, how much better it would be to have the relative merits of both positions (and others) studied openly and critically in the same class. This kind of rational comparative examination can hardly fail to be valuable and illuminating for potential teachers. The activity might appropriately be called 'philosophy of education', though what it is called is ultimately of little consequence. Teachers should be not just technicians, but highly educated people: if they are not highly educated, pupils will lose out. An important part of the education of teachers has to be the development of a critical capacity to consider the nature of education, the function of schools and their own roles within them, and educational policy at all levels.

The study of education may not sit comfortably with the conception of a teacher as someone who implements other people's policies. This is a tension that teachers have to live with: historically, a natural response to the situation has been for them to band together into groups designed to influence government thinking. Instead of dismissing such pressure as invariably springing from professional self-interest, we should worry when teachers have nothing to say about educational policy. Equally we (public and teachers) should be suspicious of governments which seek to reject or belittle educational theory. This kind of dismissiveness is far from novel: consequently the warning has been issued before. But like most important points it bears restatement.

Where a professional group has manifestly acquired a sophisticated critical understanding about X, it is hard to deny its right to exercise authoritative influence over how X is conducted. This link between learning and power underlies the perennial irritation displayed towards such groups by the political establishment. In 1879 it was expressed in a different context and a different language by Henry Craik, who became Secretary of the 'Scotch' Education Department:

> A sudden and large increase of their emoluments and an enlarged sphere of activity seem to have induced our elementary teachers to form rather an exaggerated idea of their own importance . . . .
>
> This ignorance on the part of teachers as to their position . . . is a point about which no reticence need be shown . . . . Pretensions such as those which [the teacher] sometimes puts forth – as the critic of legislation, the adviser of the Department in regard to its code, the dictator to parents of what their children shall learn, and the guide and Mentor to the School Board – must be checked and crushed without mercy . . . .
>
> The pedagogue has long been insisting that everyone should recognise the profound importance of his art . . . . He has developed a full-blown science, of which it appears he is at once the founder, the teacher, and the practical exponent; and he has got a splendid name for it. It is the 'Science of Pedagogy'. [Teachers] have besieged the Treasury and Parliament with requests for a grant to found Professorships in the Scotch Universities to teach this newly discovered, but apparently essential, science.
>
> (quoted in Stocks, 1986, p. 112)

Today we again have a government which aims to limit the power of the teaching profession and also to limit the critical study of education. It has already created both the climate and the framework within which every teacher must now think and work: both climate and framework are inimical to the child-centred tradition which this book has been concerned to restate and which many primary teachers have viewed with varying degrees of sympathy and enthusiasm.

The governments view of education has met with relatively little that could count as an adequate challenge: if teacher training is recast along the lines suggested, the possibility of such a challenge is in danger of being removed altogether. Without some introduction to progressive educational thinking, the next generation of teachers may be acquainted with no conception of education beyond an imposed curriculum made up of ten school subjects.

REFERENCES

Where the dates appear for the same item, the first indicates the date of original publication, and the second indicates the date of the edition used by the present writer. Page references given in the text refer to the later edition.

Aitkin, M., Bennett, N. and Hesketh, J. (1981) Teaching styles and pupil progress: a re-analysis, *British Journal of Educational Psychology*, Vol. 51, no. 2, pp. 170–86.

Alexander, R. (1992) *Policy and Practice in Primary Education*, Routledge, London.

Alexander, R., Rose, J. and Woodhead, C. (1992) *Curriculum Organization and Classroom Practice in Primary Schools*. A discussion paper, Department of Education and Science, London.

Archambault, R. D. (ed.) (1965) *Philosophical Analysis and Education*, Routledge & Kegan Paul, London.

Ashton, P., Kneen, P. and Holley, B. (1975) *The Aims of Primary Education*, Macmillan, London.

Aspin, D. (1984) Metaphor and meaning in educational discourse, in W. Taylor (ed.) *Metaphors of Education*, Heinemann, London.

Auld, R. (1976) *William Tyndale Junior and Infants Schools Public Inquiry: A Report to the Inner London Education Authority by Robin Auld, QC*, ILEA, London.

Ayer, A. J. (1936) (1962) *Language, Truth and Logic*, Gollancz, London.

Bantock, G. H. (1965) *Education and Values: essays in the theory of education*, Faber, London.

Bantock, G. H. (1969) Discovery methods, in C. B. Cox and A. E. Dyson (eds.) *Black Paper Two*, Critical Quarterly Society, London.

Barrow, R. (1982) Five commandments for the eighties, *Educational Analysis*, Vol. 4, no. 1, pp. 49–54.

Bassey, M. (1978) *Nine Hundred Primary School Teachers*, National Foundation for Educational Research, Windsor.

Benn;, S. I. and Peters, R. S. (1959) *Social Principles and the Democratic State*, Allen & Unwin, London.

Bennett, N. (1976a) *Teaching Styles and Pupil Progress*, Open Books, London.

Bennett, N. (1976b) Formal Challenge, *The Guardian*, 26 April.

Berlin, I. (1961) (1967) Does political theory still exist?, in P. Laslett and W. G. Runciman (eds.) *Philosophy, Politics and Society* (second series), Blackwell, Oxford.

Body, A. H. (1936) *John Wesley and Education*, Epworth, London.

Boyd, W. (1921) (1952) *The History of Western Education*, Adam & Charles Black, London.

Boyd, W. (ed.) (1930) *Towards a New Education*. Report of the Fifth World Conference of the New Education Fellowship, Knopf, London.

Boyd, W. and Rawson, W. (1965) *The Story of the New Education*, Heinemann, London.

Browne, J. D. (1987) Training the teachers: the colleges of education and the expansion of primary schooling, in R. Lowe (ed.) *The Changing Primary School*, Falmer Press, London.

Bruce, M. G. (1985) Teacher education since 1944: providing the teachers and controlling the providers, *British Journal of Educational Studies*, Vol. 33, no. 2, pp. 164–72.

CACE (Central Advisory Council for Education) (1967) *Children and their Primary Schools* (the Plowden Report), HMSO, London.

Callaghan, J. (1976) Extracts from James Callaghan's speech at Ruskin College, Oxford, 18 October 1976, in B. Moon, P. Murphy and J. Raynor (eds.) (1989) *Policies for the Curriculum*, Hodder & Stoughton, London.

Campbell, A. E. (ed.) (1938) *Modern Trends in Education*. Report of the Proceedings of the New Education Fellowship Conference held in New Zealand in July 1937, Whitcombe & Tombs, Wellington.

Child, H. A. T. (ed.) (1962) *The Independent Progressive School*, Hutchinson, London.

Chitty, C. (1989) *Towards a New Education: The Victory of the New Right?* Falmer Press, Lewes.

Consultative Committee, Board of Education (1931) *The Primary School* (the Hadow Report), HMSO, London.

Consultative Committee on the Curriculum (1987) *Curriculum Design for the Secondary Stages: Guidelines for Headteachers*, Scottish Curriculum Development Service, Dundee.

COPE (Committee on Primary Education) (1983) *Primary Education in the Eighties*, Consultative Committee on the Curriculum, Dundee.

Coveney, P. (1967) *The Image of Childhood*, Penguin, Harmondsworth.

Cox, C. B. (1992) *The Great Betrayal*, Chapman, London.

Cox, C. B. and Boyson, R. (eds.) (1975) *The Fight for Education: Black Paper 1975*, Dent, London.

Cox, C. B. and Boyson, R. (eds.) (1977) *Black Paper 1977*, Maurice Temple Smith Ltd, London.

Cox. C. B. and Dyson, A. E. (eds.) (1969a) *Fight for Education: A Black Paper* Critical Quarterly Society, London.

Cox, C. B. and Dyson, A. E. (eds.) (1969b) *Black Paper Two*, Critical Quarterly Society, London.

Cox, C. B. and Dyson, A. E. (eds.) (1970) *Black Paper Three: Goodbye Mr Short* Critical Quarterly Society, London.

Cremin, L. (1961) *The Transformation of the School: Progressivism in American Education 1876–1957*, Alfred A. Knopf, New York.

Croall, J. (1983) *Neill of Summerhill: the permanent rebel*, Routledge & Kegan Paul, London.

Cross, R. C. and Woozley, A. D. (1964) *Plato's 'Republic': A Philosophical Commentary*, Macmillan, London.

Dearden, R. F. (1967) The concept of play, in R. S. Peters (ed.) *The Concept of Education*, Routledge & Kegan Paul, London.

Dearden, R. F. (1968) *The Philosophy of Primary Education*, Routledge & Kegan Paul, London.

Dearden, R. F. (1969) The aims of primary education, in R. S. Peters (ed.) *Perspectives on Plowden*, Routledge & Kegan Paul, London.

Dearden, R. F. (1972) Education as a process of growth, in R. F. Dearden, P. H. Hirst and R. S. Peters (eds.) (1975) *A Critique of Current Educational Aims*, Routledge & Kegan Paul, London.

Dearden, R. F. (1976) *Problems in Primary Education*, Routledge & Kegan Paul, London.

Dearden, R. F., Hirst, P. H. and Peters, R. S. (eds.) (1975) *A Critique of Current Educational Aims*, Routledge & Kegan Paul, London (originally published in 1972 as the first part of *Education and the Development of Reason*).

DES (Department of Education and Science) (1985) *Better Schools*, HMSO, London.

Dewey, J. (1897) *My Pedagogic Creed*, in R. D. Archambault (ed.) (1974) *John Dewey on Education*, University of Chicago Press, Chicago.

Dewey, J. (1900) *The School and Society*, University of Chicago Press, Chicago.

Dewey, J. (1916) (1961) *Democracy and Education*, Macmillan, New York.

Downie, R. S., Loudfoot, E. and Telfer, E. (1974) *Education and Personal Relationships*, Methuen, London.

Elliott, R. K. (1984) Metaphor, imagination and conceptions of education, in W. Taylor (ed.) *Metaphors of Education*, Heinemann, London.

Ellis, T., McWhirter, J., McColgan, D., Haddow, B. (1976) *William Tyndale: the teachers' story*, Writers and Readers Publishing Cooperative, London.

Farquharson, E. (1984) *The Primary Memorandum Revisited*. M.Ed. thesis, University of Dundee.

Farquharson, E. (1985) The making of the Primary Memorandum, *Scottish Educational Review*, Vol. 17, no. 1, pp. 23–32.

Flew, A. (ed.) (1951) *Essays on Logic and Language*, Blackwell, Oxford.

Froebel, F. (1826) (1893) *The Education of Man*, Appleton, New York.

Froebel, F. (1840) (1896) *Pedagogics of the Kindergarten*, Appleton, New York.

Galton, M. (1987) Change and continuity in the primary school: the research evidence, *Oxford Review of Education*, Vol. 13, no. 1.

Galton, M., Simon, B. and Croll, P. (1980) *Inside the Primary Classroom*, Routledge & Kegan Paul, London.

Gammage, P. (1987) Chinese Whispers, *Oxford Review of Education*, Vol. 13, no. 1, pp. 95–110.

Gellner, E. (1985) *The Psychoanalytic Movement*, Paladin, London.

Green, J. A. (ed.) (1912) *Pestalozzi's Educational Writings*, Edward Arnold, London.

Gretton, J. and Jackson, M. (1976) *William Tyndale: Collapse of a School – or a System?* Allen & Unwin, London.

Grevon, P. J. (1973) *Child-Rearing Concepts 1628–1861*, F. E. Peacock, Itasca, Illinois.

Gruber, K. H. (1987) The impact of Plowden in Germany and Austria, *Oxford Review of Education*, Vol. 13, no. 1, pp. 57–66.

Halsey, A. H. and Sylva, K. (1987) Plowden: history and prospect, *Oxford Review of Education*, Vol. 13, no. 1, pp. 3–12.

Hirst, P. H. (1966) Educational theory, in J. W. Tibble (ed.) *The Study of Education*, Routledge & Kegan Paul, London.

Hirst, P. H. (1974) *Knowledge and the Curriculum*, Routledge & Kegan Paul, London.

Hirst, P. H. (1986) Richard Peters's contribution to the philosophy of education, in D. Cooper. (ed.) *Education, Values and Mind: essays for R. S. Peters*, Routledge and Kegan Paul, London.

Hirst, P. H. and Peters, R. S. (1970) *The Logic of Education*, Routledge & Kegan Paul, London.

Hoggart, R. *et al.* (1969) *The Permissive Society: The 'Guardian' Inquiry*, Panther Books, London.

Holmes, E. (1911) *What Is and What Might Be*, Constable, London.

Homan, R. (1982) What the reading lists tell us, *Times Educational Supplement* 25 June, p. 27.

Illich, I. (1973) *Deschooling Society*, Penguin, Harmondsworth.

Jacks, H. B. (1962) Bedales School in H. A. T. Child (ed.) *The Independent Progressive School*, Hutchinson, London.

Jones, D. (1987) Planning for progressivism: the changing primary school in the Leicestershire authority during the Mason era, 1947–71, in R. Lowe (ed.) *The Changing Primary School*, Falmer Press, London.

Kilpatrick, W. H. (1916) *Froebel's Kindergarten Principles Critically Examined*, Macmillan, London.

Kilpatrick, W. H. (1918) The project method, *Teachers College Record*, No. 19, pp. 319–35.

Kirk, G. (1982) *Curriculum and Assessment in the Scottish Secondary School*, Ward Lock Educational, London.

Kogan, M. (1987) The Plowden Report twenty years on, *Oxford Review of Education*, Vol. 13, no. 1, pp. 13–22.

Laslett, P. (1956) *Philosophy, Politics and Society*, Vol. I, Blackwell, Oxford.

Lilley, I. (ed.) (1967) *Friedrich Froebel: A Selection from his Writings*, Cambridge University Press.

Lunt, N., McKenzie, P. and Powell, P. (1993) The right track: teacher training and the new right: change and review, *Education Studies*, Vol. 19, no. 2, pp. 143–61.

Mackenzie, R. F. (1970) *State School*, Penguin, Harmondsworth.

Osborne, G. (1966) *Scottish and English Schools*, Longman, London.

Passow, A. H. (1982) John Dewey's influence, *Teachers College Record*, Vol. 83, no. 3, pp. 401–18.

PDC (Programme Directing Committee) (1986) *Education 10–14 in Scotland*, Dundee College of Education for the Consultative Committee on the Curriculum, Dundee.

Pestalozzi, J. (1802) (1894) *How Gertrude Teaches her Children* (trans. L. Holland and F. C. Turner) Swan Sonnenschein, London.

Pestalozzi, J. (1826) (1976) Pestalozzi's theoretical and practical method for elementary education and instruction, *Samtliche Werke*, Vol. 28, Orell Fussli Verlag, Zurich.

Peters, R. S. (1958) *The Concept of Motivation*, Routledge & Kegan Paul, London.

Peters, R. S. (1959) (1973) *Authority, Responsibility and Education*, Allen & Unwin, London.

Peters, R. S. (1963) Education as initiation, in R. S. Archambault (ed.) (1965) *Philosophical Analysis and Education*, Routledge & Kegan Paul, London.

Peters, R. S. (1964) The place of philosophy in the training of teachers, in R. S. Peters (ed.) (1977) *Education and the Education of Teachers*, Routledge & Kegan Paul, London.

Peters, R. S. (1966a) *Ethics and Education*, Allen & Unwin, London.
Peters, R. S. (1966b) The philosophy of education, in J. W. Tibble (ed.) *The Study of Education*, Routledge & Kegan Paul, London.
Peters, R. S. (ed.) (1967) *The Concept of Education*, Routledge & Kegan Paul, London.
Peters, R. S. (1969) A recognizable philosophy of education: a constructive critique, in R. S. Peters (ed.) *Persepctives on Plowden*, Routledge & Kegan Paul, London.
Peters, R. S. (1972) *Reason, Morality and Religion*, Friends Home Service Committee, London.
Peters, R. S. (1983) Philosophy of education 1960–80, in P. H. Hirst (ed.) *Educational Theory and its Foundation Discipline*, Routledge & Kegan Paul, London.
Powell, J. (1985) *The Teacher's Craft*, Scottish Council for Research in Education, Edinburgh.
Punch, M. (1973) *Dartington Hall School*. Ph.D. thesis, University of Essex.
Rawson, W. (ed.) (1933) *A New World in the Making: An International Survey of the New Education*, New Education Fellowship, London.
Rogers, V. and Barron, J. (1976) Questioning the evidence, *Times Educational Supplement*, 30 April, p. 20.
Rousseau, J.-J. (1762) (1911) *Emile* (trans. B. Foxley), Dent, London.
Schools Council (1967) *Society and the Young School Leaver*, Working Paper No. 11, HMSO, London.
Scottish Office Education Department (1983) *Curriculum and Assessment in Scotland, National Guidelines: Environmental Studies 5–14*, SOED, Edinburgh.
Scruton, R. (1987) Expressionist education, *Oxford Review of Education*, Vol. 13, no. 1, pp. 39–44.
SED (Scottish Education Department) (1965) *Primary Education in Scotland* (the Primary Memorandum). HMSO, Edinburgh.
SED (Scottish Education Department) (1980) *Learning and Teaching in Primary 4 and 7: A Progress Report by Her Majesty's Inspectorate*, HMSO, Edibnurgh.
Selleck, R. J. W. (1972) *English Primary Education and the Progressives 1914–1939*, Routledge & Kegan Paul, London.
Silber, K. (1973) *Pestalozzi: The Man and his Work*, Schocken Books, New York.
Simon, B. (1980) The primary school revolution: myth or reality? in E. Fearn and B. Simon (eds.) *Education in the Sixties*, Proceedings of the 1979 Annual Conference of the History of Education Society of Great Britain.
Simon, B. (1983) The study of education as a university subject in Britain, *Studies in Higher Education*, Vol. 8, no. 1, pp. 1–13.
Simon, B. and Willcocks, S. (eds.) (1981) *Research and Practice in the Primary Classroom*, Routledge, London.
Skilbeck, M. (1984) *School-Based Curriculum Development*, Harper & Row, London.
Snook, I. A. (1972) *Indoctrination and Education*, Routledge & Kegan Paul, London.
Southey, R. (1820) *The Life of Wesley; and the Rise and Progress of Methodism*, Longman, Hurst, Rees, Orme & Brown, London.
Stocks, J. (1986) Broken links in Scottish teacher-training, *Scottish Educational Review*, Vol. 18, no. 2, pp. 110–20.
Taylor, W. (1990) Education, in F. M. L. Thompson (ed.) *The University of London and the World of Learning 1836–1986*, Hambledon Press, London.
TESS (*Times Educational Supplement Scotland*) (1988) Curriculum policy rift grows, TESS, 24 June, p. 1.

Tibble, J. W. (ed.) (1966) *The Study of Education*, Routledge & Kegan Paul, London.

van der Eyken, W. & Turner, B. (1969) *Adventures in Education*, Allen Lane, London.

Walker, D. (1977) William Tyndale, in C. B. Cox and R. Boyson (eds.) *Black Paper 1977*, Maurice Temple Smith, London.

Williams, R. (1976) *Keywords: A Vocabulary of Culture and Society*, Fontana, Glasgow.

Wilson, R. (1977) The aerial view of Parnassus, *Oxford Review of Education*, Vol. 3, no. 2, pp. 123–34.

Woodhead, M. (1987) The needs of children: is there any value in the concept? *Oxford Review of Education*, Vol. 13, no. 2, pp. 129–40.

Wragg, T. (1980) State-approved knowledge? Ten steps down the slippery slope, in M. Golby (ed.) *The Core Curriculum: Perspectives 2*, School of Education, University of Exeter.

INDEX

Printed in the United Kingdom
by Lightning Source UK Ltd.
2319